ETTA
WRIEDT

ETTA WRIEDT

One of the Greatest American Direct
Voice Mediums of the 20th Century

THE DEFINITIVE ACCOUNT

Edited by
N. RILEY HEAGERTY

Foreword by
Dr. Ken Saari

WHITE CROW

www.whitecrowbooks.com

Etta Wriedt

A CIP catalogue record for this book is available from the British Library.
For information, contact White Crow Books by e-mail: info@whitecrowbooks.com.

Cover Design by Astrid@Astridpaints.com
Interior design by Velin@Perseus-Design.com

Paperback: ISBN: 978-1-78677-258-9
eBook: ISBN: 978-1-78677-259-6

Non-Fiction / Body, Mind & Spirit / Afterlife and Reincarnation

www.whitecrowbooks.com

Dedicated to preserving the legacy of the great mediums and the noble spirit teams that worked with them to uplift humanity, and to all those who are searching for Spiritual Truths.
May these glorious events aid you on your journey.

Also by the author

The Direct Voice: The Mediumship of Elizabeth Blake (2017).
Spectral Evidence: Mind Blowing Wonders Within The Heyday of Historic Spiritualism Vol. I (2017).
Spectral Evidence: Mind Blowing Wonders Within The Heyday of Historic Spiritualism Vol. II (2018).
Wizards of The North: The Brothers Davenport: The World Renowned Spiritual Mediums (2019).
The Hereafter: Firsthand Reports from The Frontiers of The Afterlife (2020).
The Phenomena of Spirit Materialization (2021).
Spectral Evidence: Mind Blowing Wonders Within The Heyday of Historic Spiritualism Vol. III (2022).
Portraits from Beyond: The Mediumship of the Bangs Sisters (2016).
The French Revelation (1995 & 2015).

SOLITUDE
Ella Wheeler Wilcox

Laugh, and the world laughs with you;
Weep, and you weep alone,
For the sad old earth must borrow its mirth,
But has trouble enough of its own.

Sing, and the hills will answer;
Sigh, it is lost on the air,
The echoes bound to a joyful sound,
But shrink from voicing care.

Rejoice, and men will seek you;
Grieve, and they turn and go,
They want full measure of all your pleasure,
But they do not need your woe.
Be glad and your friends are many;
Be sad, and you lose them all,
There are none to decline your nectar'd wine,
But alone you must drink life's gall.

Feast, and your halls are crowded;
Fast, and the world goes by,
Succeed and give, and it helps you live,
But no man can help you die.

There is room in the halls of pleasure;
For a large and lordly train,
But one by one we must all file on,
Through the narrow aisles of pain.

Portrait of Etta Wriedt
by Helen G. Smith.
Courtesy of The College of Psychic Studies, London

ACKOWLEDGEMENTS

~

There are many of whom I wish to thank for aiding me in this unforgettable adventure and, I want to add, a goodly bunch of them made involved, valiant efforts but actually failed to find any reliable information for me involving Etta Wriedt, but nonetheless, they certainly tried. Melissa Cornelius, the Oswego City Librarian, for her *enormous* help in finding local information on Etta, her parents and their history; The College of Psychic Studies, London, England; The Churchill Archives Center, University of Cambridge, England; Johanna Ward and Domniki Papadimitriou, Picture Library Assistant, Cambridge University Library, England; The Detroit Public Library; The Spiritualist Association of Great Britain; National Archives of Canada; Angela Burgess at the Evergreen Cemetery, Detroit, who took photos of the mausoleum plaque; Charles Klepadlo, Historian, Camp Chesterfield, Indiana, for the photo of the auditorium plaque; Peter Johnson, Society of Psychical Research, London; Dayton Metro Library, Ohio; The Genealogy Center, Fort Wayne, Indiana; The Society of Psychic Research, England; Dr. Ken Saari, a friend and fellow explorer for writing the Foreword; to the amazing August Goforth,[1] for formatting and designing my previous seven books and adding invaluable insight throughout; Jon Beecher, Publisher of White Crow Books, a true comrade and friend and last but not least, ever, my beloved wife and soul comrade, Caroline Robertson-Heagerty, she is all the inspiration I will ever need.

---

[1] See *The Risen,* by August Goforth, an outstanding work. 2009.

Although many of the messages expressed within this book were spoken over 100 years ago, they are not the words of the so-called dead, but of the still-vibrant intelligences of those who never died and continue to live. But don't take my word for it—we each must listen to and consider the stories of these individuals within one's own consciousness, to experience and gain the evidence that will be of unique significance to you and you alone—until you will surely come to realize that no matter how much you might think you are, you are never alone. *The stories of life within this incalculably valuable book can only strengthen the realization that our loved ones are never very far away, but closer than we could ever imagine.*

~ AUGUST, GOFORTH,
AUTHOR OF *THE RISEN: DIALOGUES OF LOVE, GRIEF, & SURVIVAL BEYOND DEATH* AND
THE RISEN: A COMPANION TO GRIEF

CONTENTS

~

FOREWORD

~

It was at a very young age when I first began to think about dying. The thought of being placed in a box and being buried deep beneath the ground for the rest of eternity was, to this day, the most terrifying thought that I have ever had. I think I was six or seven years old at the time and I can still vividly remember lying in bed trembling and crying hysterically as I pulled the covers over my head. Since that night, I have spent a lifetime searching for any scraps of evidence that could indicate that there might be an afterlife. I had to find out.

Fast forward to circa 2003. I was in a used bookstore in Fort Worth, Texas, with my wife and three children. We routinely took the kids to bookstores where each one of us would pick out a book to read. Reading being the true foundation for learning, we strenuously encouraged it in our family. I immediately gravitated to the metaphysics/parapsychology section of the store and perused the volumes for something interesting. A short time later, my daughter called out to me to advise me that they were already at the checkout counter and that I should hurry and come join them. Not having selected a book yet, I decided to close my eyes and pull out the first one that I put my fingers on. It was a book called *The Dead Are Alive*, by Harold Sherman. I was halfway through the second chapter when I came to the definitive realization that we do indeed survive death. What a life altering epiphany! My thinking, based on intense reflection at that time was: "You just can't make this stuff up." The more I read, the more accepting I was of the evidence, which I found to be irrefutable and in great supply.

Fast forward again to 2007. Now, I am really on a roll. I have been reading anything and everything I could get my hands on involving the subject of survival. A dear friend, who was also on this afterlife investigation journey with me had read and most highly recommended a book titled: *The French Revelation* by N. Riley Heagerty. This was Heagerty's first book and changed my life more than any other. For me, this 'sealed the deal' so to speak. Since then, I have read all nine of Heagerty's life altering books about the most highly developed physical mediums of the past hundred and fifty years.

This leads me to his latest book; a brilliant and comprehensive biographical account of the life and mediumship of one of the greatest direct voice trumpet mediums ever to grace the shores of the United States. Her name was Etta Wriedt.

Once again, Heagerty has, after an exhaustive and lengthy period of investigation and research, brilliantly presented a most splendid and comprehensive biographical account of this truly remarkable medium who possessed the "right stuff" that allowed her to bring forth frequent and extensive verbal communication with people on the other side whom society labels as dead.

Born on December 10, 1862, Etta Wriedt went on to become one of the greatest direct voice mediums during that time period, in the world. Direct voice means that the spirit voices come through independent of the medium and are heard several feet from the medium. The voices are transmitted through an aluminum megaphone, usually about twenty inches long, which is commonly referred to as a trumpet. She was however much more than just a trumpet medium. As astounding as direct voice mediumship is, she was also a physical medium. Many times during a demonstration, those in attendance would witness levitation of objects in the room and apports-objects brought into the room by spirit operators and left behind. Through her mediumship, she was also able to produce on certain occasions, etherealizations and materializations.

Etherializations are spirit people who are able to manifest in their etheric or energy bodies which are transparent but nonetheless discernible, as opposed to materializations which are solid and three dimensional.

On numerous occasions, attendees were able to embrace their loved ones and engage in conversation which left them with no doubt whatsoever regarding the continuity of life and the reality of spirit return. Throughout her life, through her mediumship, she was able to reunite countless numbers of sitters with their departed loved ones who were able to provide irrefutable evidence of their identity, thus confirming to their loved ones that they are indeed still very much alive.

Etta traveled extensively and held demonstrations of her abilities for more than forty years. Throughout her many years as a practicing medium, she met many important and influential people while traveling abroad including Sir Arthur Conan Doyle, Sir Oliver Lodge, Sir William Barrett, Admiral Osborne Moore, and even developed a close friendship with Queen Victoria for whom she had sittings. Throughout her life, she provided many sittings for many of these luminaries. During these demonstrations, Wriedt would never be in an altered state of consciousness or what is known as a 'trance state.' She was always consciously aware of what was transpiring and was able to participate in the conversations with the so called dead. On many occasions the sitters heard her and a spirit communicator speaking at the same time. Frequently, sitters were able to hear two or three spirit communicators speaking simultaneously. During one demonstration, the sitters were able to hear four spirit communicators all speaking at the same time, and in different languages. What is most astounding and evidential is the fact that Wriedt could only speak one language— English. Over the years, spirit communicators came through speaking fourteen different languages—further evidence of the reality of spirit communication and survival.

A great deal of gratitude must go to the author, who arduously, steadfastly and tirelessly pursued a trail of leads in locating and investigating any and all information regarding the life and mediumship of this true 'Wonder of the World'—Etta Wriedt. This book, as with all of his books, must be savored like a fine wine, to truly appreciate and assimilate the Earth shattering marvels of this extremely gifted medium. This book is profoundly life changing, and is yet another great addition to his brilliant compilation of nine outstanding books and adds greatly to the ever increasing body of irrefutable afterlife evidence.

Dr. Ken Saari
Vienna

INTRODUCTION

~

"Nature has planted in our minds an
insatiable longing to see the truth."

~ Marcus Tullius Cicero

M rs. Henrietta 'Etta' Wriedt, the subject of this work and one of the greatest direct voice mediums in the history of Modern Spiritualism was born, Henrietta Knapp, in my own birthplace and hometown of Oswego, New York, on December 10th, 1862. She resided at 20 West 8th Street, ninety years before I was born on East Sixth Street. I have been aware of Etta for decades and have never been surprised that she was born on one of the Great Lakes-Lake Ontario – the literal northern side of the city of Oswego itself, and when she settled in Michigan, she was almost directly in the middle of three of these mighty water bodies: Lake Erie, Huron and Michigan. In my previous book, *Portraits From Beyond*, 2016, in the Appendices I included a section, "The Spirit Zone of The Northeast," in which I listed an absolutely staggering amount of the greatest and most powerful American physical mediums who all lived and practiced in this psychic powerhouse area of the United States.

The spirits had said that this geographical area, with its cool, crisp, dry atmosphere and the outstanding abundance of electrical energy was perfect for the manifestation of spirit phenomena, especially of the physical nature. These facts certainly spoke for themselves as I slowly unearthed all of the mediums that I have, one by one, over these many years. It is a very simple concept concerning research: stay true to your mission and never give up. It took me almost six initial years of research and book hunting to suddenly come upon the fact that Etta was from Oswego, thanks to a 1930's edition of *Hartmann's Who's Who in Occult, Psychic and Spiritual Realms* that I located, around 1995, in a small, cozy, used bookstore in the outback of the Pennsylvania, Amish hills. That bookstore, *The Owl* which, to me, became over time like an old friend, eventually was put out of business—as many of them were—by the advancing charge of the internet. There are still rare, used bookstores out there, let's hope they stay around. The long, hopeful journey's to the old establishments in search of Spiritualist gems are memories that will stay with me forever and I will always keep searching.

I know from doing this research for decades that I am a rare breed. I feel compelled to do this work, I feel that *someone* has to. There are others, like Mike Tymn, Ron Nagy and Shannon Taggert who are also involved in this amazing form of research who's work I deeply respect. [2]

With Open Arms

In my opinion, many individuals, unaware of the data, seem to think that as far as the subject of spirits, séances and mediums are concerned, it's "history" so-called, is only relevant to and created by the experiences of people in modern times. The past records of Spiritualism seem to be inconsequential to them because it's not part of the present. This, of course, is preposterous and lends itself to the theory that people will base their beliefs only on what they themselves literally experience, and the past history is something that does not matter *now*. I understand this to a certain extent because the evidence for life after death is still a hard sell for many in any context, but they might not be aware of the outstanding and marvelous records of what individuals have witnessed and the teachings that were documented during the 'heyday' of what is essentially Victorian (Historic) Spiritualism, which I put between

---

[2] See *Séance*, by Shannon Taggert, 2022, and *The Articulate Dead*, 2008, by Michael E. Tymn, one of many of his published works, and *Precipitated Spirit Paintings*, 2006, and *The Spirits of Lily Dale*, 2011, by Ron Nagy and the late Joyce Lajudice.

1848 and 1955-60 and is one of the most important bodies of work ever put on this earth.

Unfortunately, most people will never have a chance to be transformed by a mediumistic event, one that changes the entire landscape of their thinking and beliefs. So, having said that, I believe that the records of Historic Spiritualism, one shining gem of which involves the medium this work is about, Etta Wriedt, can change the dynamics of your thinking. Based on the deep integrity of the witnesses and the sheer volume of the documentation, *it's simply too impossible not to believe*. These events should be a form of liberation, a life altering experience to rational human beings.

These following pages-and I say this as a researcher, archivist and author of thirty years-contain the proof of life after death and spirit return. Allow yourself to balance the facts within the Court of Common Sense. It may liberate your mind and make you fearless, for you will know for certain that you are *forever*, eternal, and the boundless Universe stands majestically before you, with open arms.

The Supreme Hierarchy

To this researcher, there are two outstanding mediums I would rank within the Supreme Hierarchy of Trumpet Mediumship (Direct-Voice), and that is first, hands down, Elizabeth Blake (1847-1920), and secondly, Etta Wriedt (1862-1942). In the case of Mrs. Blake, for the sheer longevity of her career, sixty years, the iron-clad evidential power of the spirit messages and, unless proven otherwise, *not one* recorded instance of a blank séance, or sitting, she sits at the top of the list. The aspect of fame was not of interest to her although she was more famous that she could possibly comprehend. I had discovered, in the course of researching her life that she had never ventured more than two miles from her humble cottage in Bradrick, Ohio, on the banks of the Ohio River in her entire life. She was a wonder of the world and chose, ever so humbly, to be a homebody. With Etta, fame seemed to follow her, and she went with it, in both America, and Europe, where she was held in the highest regard, and rightly so.

I have felt the need over many years to bring forward an entire book on the remarkable Mrs. Wriedt. There are definitive works that have been done concerning her seances[3] and these I have held as treasures in my library for decades. In light of this, I decided to publish a book that would include many of the most outstanding instances of these previous works I mentioned, and also add biographical and historical items that have, at large, never been made public. There was more than a sufficient amount of documented séance memoranda involving Etta Wriedt which is still incredible, especially for enthusiasts of this subject-but, as with most of the great mediums from Historic Spiritualism, it was really a challenge finding information about Mrs. Wriedt's personal life. I have included a significant amount of material from W. Usborne Moore who, without question, did humanity an outstanding service by documenting, more than anyone in the history of Spiritualism, so much information and séance memoranda involving this psychic wonderworker. The complete Introduction to his book, *The Voices*, I have included further on in this work owing to its phenomenal importance.

---

[3] See: *Psychic Experiences Throughout the World,* by Ernest A. S. Hayward, Rider & Company, London, 1939, extremely rare; *The Voices*, by W. Usborne Moore, London, Watts & Company 1913; *Glimpses of The Next State,* London, Watts & Company, 1911; *Dawn of The Awakened Mind* by John S. King M.D., The James A. McCann Company, New York, 1920; *This World and Beyond,* by Mrs. Philip Champion De Crespigny, Cassell & Company, London, 1934; *Man's Survival After Death*, by Charles L. Tweedale, Richards, London, 1909; Arthur Conan Doyle, *The New Revelation,* Hodder and Stoughton, London, 1918; Has W. T. Stead Returned? By James Coates, L. N. Fowler, England, 1913.

1

ETTA IN THE NEWS

~

*"Whatever the humblest of men affirm from their own experience is
always worth listening to, but what even the cleverest of men, in their
ignorance, deny, is never worth a moment's attention."*

~ SIR WILLIAM BARRETT

Concerning Oswego, New York, Etta was the daughter of Henry Van Buren Knapp and Elizabeth Creed and they were part of the O'Keefee/Hannegan family tree. Thanks to Melissa Cornelius at the Oswego Public Library, we found out that Etta, soon after she was born in 1862 went with her mother to Canada after she had separated from Van Buren Knapp who, being a 'boatsman' stayed in Oswego, being the seafaring area that it was and still is. Etta's sister, Mary Ann Knapp was born in Canada one year after Etta was born. I was able to find out that Elizabeth Creed was born in 1840, Newfoundland, Labrador, Canada, and passed away in Missouri, USA., the date of which is currently unknown. Moving forward, I do know that Etta was living as a single woman in Dayton View, Ohio at 311 North Salem Street by 1886, at twenty-four years old. She was married to Phillip Knapp on August 1, 1889, in Montgomery, Ohio, which then puts her at twenty-seven years old. She was widowed in 1930 after forty years of marriage to Phillip and she passed to spirit in Detroit, on September 14, 1942, at 2108 Baldwin Avenue. Etta was 80 years, nine months and three days old at her transition to that wondrous world of spirits she knew so well. Her full name Henrietta George Knapp Wriedt and she signed her passport application as Etta George Wriedt.

THE *DETROIT NEWS*, 1942
THE PASSING OF ETTA WRIEDT
TOWN TALK
George W. Stark: Reporter

"Not alone because she was the sole possessor of the Victoria watch, but because she was in her day the Number One spiritualist medium in the world, will the fame of Mrs. Etta Wriedt rest. Mrs. Wriedt has now experienced that change which we call death and the end came to her quietly at her home, 2108 Baldwin Avenue. Services will be conducted Thursday afternoon at the Curtiss Funeral Home, at Jefferson and Parker Avenues. She will be buried in Evergreen Cemetery. She was born in Oswego, New York, 80 years ago and lived in Detroit 45 years.

"Etta Wriedt's later days were filled with peace and serenity. It wasn't always thus. In her younger days, when she exercised her mastery of séance technique's, here and in England, she endured both lavish praise and cynical criticism, both with equanimity. She may well have been proud of her endorsements which came from a such a distinguished clientele as Sir Arthur Conan Doyle, Admiral Osborne Moore, and William T. Stead. It was generally agreed that it was Etta Wriedt who established spirit communication between Sir Arthur and his son. She was always very modest about her part. But when Sir Arthur was here in 1922, he told an astonished newspaper man that Detroit was unaware that it was the home of the world's greatest medium, Mrs. Wriedt. But you'll want to know about the Victoria watch, a dramatic symbol of Etta Wriedt's amazing powers, which is now in the possession of the council of the London Spiritualist Alliance. The Victoria watch was first given by the Queen to Miss Georgiana Eagle[4] for her extraordinary

---

[4] Georgiana Eagle (1835-1911) Georgiana Eagle was a female magician and psychic performer during the mid-1800's in Europe.

clairvoyance. This was in 1846, when the Queen was 25 years old and had been on the throne nine years.

"Nobody seems to know what became of the watch after it passed from the possession of Miss Eagle, but it was finally owned by William T. Stead, in whose London home, Etta Wriedt, in 1911, gave a series of sittings. He was so enthusiastic about the results of these that he presented her the famous watch. Mr. Stead was on his way to America the following year to escort Mrs. Wriedt to England again for a new series of séances, when he met his death in the Titanic disaster.

"Later, Mrs. Wriedt presented the watch to the London Spiritualist Alliance, where it could be kept as a memorial to the authenticity of Spiritualism and to the consuming interest the great English Queen professed in it. The watch bears two noteworthy inscriptions: *Presented by Her Majesty to Miss Georgiana Eagle for her meritorious and extraordinary clairvoyance produced at Osborne House, Isle of Wight, July 15, 1846.* And *Presented by W. T. Stead to Mrs. Etta Wriedt, through whose mediumship Queen Victoria's voice was heard in London in July, 1911.*

"Etta Wriedt was never boastful of her powers. She shunned publicity and was extremely sensitive of the criticism leveled at Spiritualism.

"I never talk about myself," she once told a reporter. "I will let the things I have accomplished for various people speak for me. Those who are in sympathy with the spirit know me, those who are out of sympathy do not need to know me.

THE *DETROIT FREE PRESS*
SEPTEMBER 15th, 1945
MRS. ETTA WRIEDT,
SPIRITUALIST, SUCCUMBS

"Mrs. Etta Wriedt, world celebrated Spiritualist and one time friend of Queen Victoria, died Sunday at her home at 2018 Baldwin Avenue. She was born in Oswego, New York, 80 years ago and had lived in Detroit for 45 years.

"She was a member of the *Order of The Eastern Star* and Psychical Research Society of London and New York. Services will be held at the Curtiss Funeral Home, 8045 East Jefferson, at 2pm Thursday. Burial will be in Evergreen Mausoleum.

"A collaborator with Sir Oliver Lodge and Arthur Conan Doyle, Mrs. Wriedt made several trips to England. She was a cousin of Lloyd George. For her work as a Spiritualist she was presented with the watch of Queen Victoria in London in 1911. She recently had returned the watch to the Duchess of Hamilton."

The Order of the Eastern Star was a Masonic appendant body open to both men and women. It was established in 1850 (172 years ago) by lawyer and educator Rob Morris, a noted Freemason, and adopted and approved as an appendant body of the Masonic Fraternity in 1873. The order is based on some teachings from the Bible, and is open to people of all religious beliefs. It has approximately 10,000 chapters in twenty countries and approximately 500,000 members under its General Grand Chapter.

Members of the Order of the Eastern Star are aged 18 and older, men must be Master Masons and women must have specific relationships with Masons. Originally, a woman would have to be the daughter, widow, wife, sister, or mother of a Master Mason. The Order now allows other relatives as well as allowing Job's Daughters, Rainbow Girls, Members of the Organization of Triangles (NY only) and members of the Constellation of Junior Stars (NY only) to become members when of age.

BY CABLE: TO THE PHILADELPHIA PUBLIC LEDGER/ BROOKLYN EAGLE BIG ADVANCE SEEN IN SPIRITUALISM 1920
American Leader in The Movement Says The War Gave it Great Impetus
London, October 5th

"Spiritualism has made remarkable progress since my last visit to England," said Mrs. Etta Wriedt of Detroit, one of the leaders of the movement in America, in an interview here.

"The war created a new field for Spiritualism," she continued, "and as a result, during the last two years the advancement has exceeded that of any previous period of equal duration. People who lost relatives and friends in the trenches and training camps in the prime of life have been unwilling to let them pass on without making an effort at communication. They have become interested in our work from spiritual and not from materialistic reasons. The average man of the world is seeking new religion."

"Spiritualism is the coming religion, which is going to take the place of the old church doctrinal belief. It has been a hard struggle, but the worst is over. We have interested an intellectual class of people who are eager to help the cause."

"In speaking of the position of Spiritualism in Europe as compared with that in the United States, Mrs. Wriedt said the people in Great Britain and France are more interested and enthusiastic than those of America, and as a result, more progress has been made in those two countries. She praised highly the work of Sir Arthur Conan Doyle and said he was appealing to the hearts and not to the pocketbooks of the people.

"When asked as to the possibility of the future use of Spiritualism in catching criminals, Mrs. Wriedt expressed the opinion that she is outside the legitimate field of the movement which is essentially a spiritual one."

The following documented, eye-witnessed accounts by Vice Admiral W. Usborne Moore is, without question, one of the most important bodies of work involving Direct Voice Phenomena ever recorded and it is an honor to include them in this work (Ed.).

2

AN HONEST ENQUIRER: VICE ADMIRAL WILLIAM USBORNE MOORE

~

"The medium, who is an uncultured person, does not know any language but Yankee, she cannot even speak proper English, yet the spirits have been heard to speak Arabic, Croatian, Servian, Dutch, French, German, Hebrew, Hindustani, Italian, Norwegian, Spanish, Welsh, Scotch, and Gaelic."

~ W. USBORNE MOORE

William Usborne Moore (March 8, 1849 – March 15, 1918) also known as W. Usborne Moore was a British naval commander, psychical researcher and Spiritualist. After Moore retired in 1904 with the rank of Rear Admiral in the British Navy, he became interested in Spiritualism. He became a fearless champion and defender of Etta Wriedt and the Bangs Sisters. Admiral Moore's expertise in naval surveying and experiences in scientific endeavors suited him perfectly in his investigations into the phenomena of spirit manifestations. He authored two books, *Glimpses of the Next State* (1911), and *The Voices,* (1913), which detailed his investigations of a number of mediums in Great Britain and the United States (Ed.).

INTRODUCTION TO *THE VOICES*

Every attempt—such as the one I am making—to bring home to mortals the knowledge of the proximity of their beloved dead must, owing to the very nature of the subject, be only partially successful. There are *five difficulties* with which I have to contend:

(1) The reluctance of people to write at all, (2) their special reluctance to put on paper details which may sooner or later give pain or offence to living friends or relatives, (3) the national habit of reserve which causes many a man to become an oyster when he thinks he may be betrayed into revealing his innermost feelings—that which deeply stirs his heart, (4) the fear of ridicule, diminution of income, loss of position, or respect of his fellow men, (5) the apprehension of appearing more credulous than his associates (perhaps the most powerful motive for silence). Thus, after all, the man who aims at obtaining the true opinions of investigators into this sacred subject only receives the rind of the fruit, the fruit itself remains untouched.

"To some extent I, the author—or, more properly, the editor—of this collection of narratives am "cribbed, cabined, and confined " by one or other of the above restrictions. Neither in *Glimpses of The Next State,* nor in this sequel, *The Voices,* have I given the whole evidence for the faith that is in me. I have submitted all I can with propriety, but there is much behind that is suppressed which, if known, would be absolutely convincing to the few, but become the subject of ignorant buffoonery to the many—to the great majority who are tied and bound by sacerdotalism[5] or materialism. However, the requests I have made to those who have had sittings with this highly-privileged woman, Mrs. Etta Wriedt, have been met with as willing a response as one can expect, considering the age in which we live, and the narratives which have been furnished me I earnestly hope may assist the weary and dispirited to take up their lives again and bravely face the future in the sure and certain hope that they will meet, at no great distance of time, with those they have lost awhile, or, at any rate, encourage

---

[5] Sacerdotalism: Religious belief emphasizing the powers of priests as essential mediators between God and humankind.

them to seek assurance for themselves by personal investigation on the same lines.

"That noble soul, W. T. Stead,[6] conceived a plan for giving comfort to the bereaved which was perfect of its kind, but the form that it took rendered it liable to extinction directly its founder passed to the higher life. But the spirit of what he created, " Julia's Bureau " still lives. It is in the power of every man and woman in comfortable circumstances to carry out the idea in their own person. Let us each do what we individually can to assist with our purse, those whom we know to be in trouble to find consolation by investigation through competent psychics. If we do this, have we not accomplished in detail, what Stead and his guide, Julia, did in wholesale fashion?

---

[6] William Thomas Stead (5 July 1849 – 15 April 1912) was a British newspaper editor who, as a pioneer of investigative journalism, became a controversial figure of the Victorian era. Stead published a series of hugely influential campaigns whilst editor of The *Pall Mall Gazette*, including his 1885 series of articles, "The Maiden Tribute of Modern Babylon." These were written in support of a bill, later dubbed the "Stead Act", that raised the age of consent from 13 to 16.

Stead's "new journalism" paved the way for the modern tabloid in Great Britain. He has been described as "the most famous journalist in the British Empire." He is considered to have influenced how the press could be used to influence public opinion and government policy, and advocated "Government by Journalism". He was known for his reportage on child welfare, social legislation and reformation of England's criminal codes.

Stead died in the sinking of the *RMS Titanic.* In the 1890s, he became increasingly interested in Spiritualism. In 1893, he founded a spiritualist quarterly, Borderland, in which he gave full play to his interest in psychical research. Stead was editor, and he employed Ada Goodrich Freer as assistant editor; she was also a substantial contributor under the pseudonym "Miss X". Stead claimed that he was in the habit of communicating with Freer by telepathy and automatic writing. The magazine ceased publication in 1897.

Stead claimed to be in receipt of messages from the spirit world and, in 1892, to be able to produce automatic writing. His spirit contact was alleged to be the departed Julia A. Ames, an American temperance reformer and journalist whom he met in 1890 shortly before her death. In 1909, he established Julia's Bureau, where inquirers could obtain information about the spirit world from a group of resident mediums. Stead was a fearless champion for the truths of Spiritualism and his name will live forever in it's ranks.

"In these days of general education it is futile to tell a man of any intelligence that he will meet his child again some millions of years hence on a Day of Judgment, when he may again part with him. He wants to know if his child is alive now, if he is happy or likely to become so, if he will be restored to him, if he will again hold him in his arms, and be to him what he was before his transition to the Next State. Whether his child was good, or whether he was bad, the parent's mind cannot grasp that he is eternally lost to him. His sense of justice revolts against the decree of the Church, and he will have none of it. It is to this man that Spiritualism appeals and it is this man that all should desire to help. And help is at hand.

"This American woman has a mysterious gift which enables those who sit in the same room with her to learn of the continued existence of those whose physical bodies have perished. The possession of this strange power is acquired by no virtue of her own, she was born with it. Unlike the gifts of poetry, art, oratory, or song, it demands from her no effort, and, with proper precautions, it causes no strain upon her physical constitution. To exhibit it, all she has to do is to sit passively in a chair, preferably in pitch darkness. It is, indeed, difficult to know what her personality has to do with the phenomena, for she never goes into the trance condition, and talks naturally throughout. What we do know is that we cannot hear a whisper when she is out of the house, but that, if she is in the room, we can distinguish voices in full light or in darkness, if in the latter, they speak louder, longer, clearer, and, in every way, more satisfactorily than in light. When the room is made pitch dark we cannot only hear the voices, but can see, as phantasms, those to whom they belong. We are told by Dr. Sharp that the power to speak is obtained from the sitters, and that they succeed or fail according to what " they are able to give out, " that some people give out freely, others not at all, and that his medium is not " drawn upon " more than is absolutely necessary. He includes me in the first category, and, if I am to judge by my feelings after a good private seance, he is correct, for I am depleted, and cannot continue investigations without long periods of rest.

"That Mrs. Wriedt is not drained is proved to my satisfaction by the following incident:—In 1913, owing to her suddenly announcing her intention to leave Cambridge House twenty-four hours before the time agreed upon, I found myself obliged to put four more sitters than was customary into the last day of her visit. In the morning she gave four private sittings, in the afternoon four, and in the evening she held a general circle of twelve people. All these seances were successful. At 10 p.m. one of the party took her to Euston in his motor, and forty-five hours later she began a series of excellent seances in Glasgow.

"Mrs. Wriedt's spirit control is Dr. John Sharp, mentioned above, who was born in Glasgow in the eighteenth century, lived all his life in the United States as an apothecary farmer, and died in Evansville, Indiana. He states that he was taken over to America by his parents when he was two months old. I have never known him say an unkind word, nor express any feeling but benevolence and desire to assist all who seek the help of his medium. He frequently straightens out obscure messages, and invariably endeavors to manage the sittings to the best advantage of those present. Very often he talks what, in a mortal, I should call nonsense, but I think he is limited in expression in some curious way—by the absence of any sort of culture in his medium. John King (Sir Henry Morgan), the control of Cecil Husk, the blind medium, frequently managed Mrs. Wriedt's seances in England.

"It was explained that he was better acquainted with English people than Dr. Sharp, who, however, was always in the background. He only put in a word or two at Rothesay. Grayfeather, a North American Indian medicine chief when in life, the control of J. B. Jonson, the materialization medium of Toledo, Ohio, U.S.A., visited me several times at Cambridge House, and often came to the circles, he seldom manifested when I was absent. He did not come to Rothesay at all. The spirits Mimi and Blossom were casual visitors. The former we know nothing about. Blossom states that in life she belonged to the Seminole tribe of Indians, who lived in the Everglades, South Florida, and that she died as a child. It is as a noisy, fractious, but extremely witty child that she now manifests. Her talk, engaging manner, and lively repartee always created a diversion, causing much laughter, which benefited conditions.

"Now and then Dr. Sharp, John King, Grayfeather, and Blossom all manifested at the same circle. When there was not sufficient power, or the proper sort of power, present for the more refined manifestation of the direct voice the controls resorted to the exhibition of the coarser physical phenomena of telekinesis, moving a table with a vase of flowers upon it, throwing trumpets about, and so forth. Occasionally these things occurred at the best of seances when the direct voices were also abundant. There were many blank seances in both years, and also some very poor ones. This is only what reasonable investigators expect in the presence of all powerful mediums, it is as provoking to the psychic as to the sitters, and some people, of whom I am one, consider it evidence of the genuineness of the proceedings.

"In 1913 a curious fact was observed. I spent thirteen or fourteen days at Cambridge House, and in the garden, from 10 a.m. to 4 or 5 p.m. On these days there were no blanks, and only two or three indifferent sittings. I am not conscious of my mind being occupied in the slightest degree with what was going on in the seance-room, nor have I any pretensions to the possession of psychic powers. But it has occurred to Miss Harper, the hostess, and to me, that it is possible my absolute conviction, after over a hundred experiments of the genuineness of Mrs. Wriedt's extraordinary gift may have, in some occult manner, found its way into the seance-room and assisted the controls. I make no assertion, but throw this speculation out to my readers as one worth consideration.

"That W. T. Stead was at the back of us, and gave us his assistance, I have no doubt whatever. In 1912 Mrs. Wriedt arrived on the evening of May 5, twenty days after his death. After her supper she proposed a seance. Stead manifested, and gave three admirable tests of his identity—two to Miss Harper,[7] and one to me, he also directly instructed us where his daughter was to sit on the following evening. The test he gave to me was unmistakable, he alluded to the conversation we had at Bank Buildings the last time I saw him. This conversation had lasted half an hour, and ranged over a variety of subjects, but the chief topic was the approaching visit of Mrs. Wriedt to his house. He desired that certain conditions should be observed, and it was to one of these conditions that his spirit referred, with emphasis, on this evening. (See *Light*, May 18, 1912, page 239.)

"The spirit called Iola in these pages is that of a lady who passed over forty years ago in the prime of her life. She was a near and dear relation of my own, and has proved herself to be so closely in touch with me that I am justified in calling her my guide."

The following account of the daily life of Etta Wriedt is a gem of research because these intimate accounts of mediums are as rare as it gets. We are fortunate to have Moore's inside look at one of the greatest mediums within the history of Historic Spiritualism especially adding the fact that he was allowed to live at her house for twenty days. A very fortunate man, indeed (Ed.).

---

[7] Mrs. E. K. Harper, W. T. Stead's secretary.

THE DAILY LIFE OF ETTA WRIEDT FROM
GLIMPSES OF THE NEXT STATE
DETROIT, 1911, W. USBORNE MOORE

"In the beautiful city of Detroit, in the State of Michigan, there are nearly half a million inhabitants. Over one third of these are intelligent Roman Catholics, conscientiously opposed to the display of psychic phenomena. In a pretty villa, built to her own design, three miles from the City Hall, lives, unmolested, Mrs. Wriedt, a so-called " trumpet medium." She has done more good, probably, than any medium in the world, in being the passive means of affording consolation to the bereaved, and in bringing hundreds to the certain knowledge of the proximity of the spirits of their relatives who have passed the change we call " death." For my part I can only say that, in her presence, I obtained evidence of the next state of consciousness so clear and so pronounced that the slightest doubt was no longer possible. I left her house in February 1911, in the condition of mind of a man who no longer fosters " belief, " but who knows what is his destiny when the tomb closes over him and his spirit leaves the earth plane.

"Mrs. Wriedt is forty-nine years of age, a slightly built, delicate woman, much subject to bronchitis and neuritis. Last year (1910) she had what she was told by the physicians was neuritis at the base of the brain, and would have died had it not been for the benevolence of Mr. C. A. Newcomb, an investigator into psychic matters, who summoned a celebrated specialist and saved her life. Since her recovery her power has been more remarkable than before her illness. I was fortunate enough to sit with her, on this, my third visit to the States, when she was in her prime as a psychic. When she heard I was in the neighborhood she wrote to me asking me to become her guest. I accepted this kind invitation, and spent twenty days in her house, where I occupied a room near the seance-room. Incidentally I may mention that I was more comfortable in this house than I was in 1909, when I put up at the two best hotels in the city.

"She keeps no servant, assisted by her husband, she does all the work of the house during intervals between her seances. In my opinion this is beneficial to her, for it completely diverts her attention from psychic matters, probably her life is wisely guided by her control, Dr. Sharp, and other good spirits. She cannot see one half the people who apply for sittings, but she does her best to give satisfaction to all, the poor are

21

often admitted for nothing. Her usual fee for each sitter is one dollar but, once a week, she gives a public seance, when nobody is expected to pay more than half-a-dollar. It is on these occasions that the poor are often invited to join the circle without paying any fee.

"Mrs. Wriedt cannot obtain phenomena when sitting by herself. About twelve years ago she was asked, as an experiment, to sit with seven deaf mutes from Flint, Michigan. No one in the room could utter an articulate word except herself. Two of the sitters were frightened because they were touched by the trumpet, no other results were obtained. Of course, it was not to be expected that the sitters would hear anything, but the point of the story is, that the psychic did not hear a word herself. If there is but one child in the room, who can prattle and hear normally, manifestations take place. My experiences with this wonderful medium in 1909 were insignificant compared with those on this, my third, visit to America. All my relatives that I wished to hear from spoke to me at some time or the other, touching upon all sorts of subjects of family interest. Lola, my spirit guide, talked daily at considerable length, often standing before me, a radiant figure in white garments but features invisible, clearly enunciating her sentences in pure English. As I have said before in my written work, Mrs. Wriedt speaks Yankee. English was not spoken by any spirit friends of American sitters. Most of my sittings were with the psychic alone, when Lola would manifest and explain matters which happened as much as fifty years ago.

"When I was a boy, a family tangle took place which puzzled me very much. Up to this time (1911) I had not even suspected the real truth. My guide, in the course of four or five interviews, solved the enigma, and brought three witnesses from spirit life who spoke at some length to prove that she was right. Dates were given and motives explained. I possessed just sufficient knowledge of what had taken place at that time to be able to assure myself-now that light was thrown upon certain incidents-that all they said was true. No one living knows anything about it except myself, but I am certain that the explanation, given with great earnestness and wealth of detail, by these visitants from the next state of consciousness, is the correct one. If I had no other experience to record in support of the doctrines of spiritualism this story, told in clear accents and exhibiting intimate knowledge of terrene life, with all its mistakes and failures, would have been sufficient to settle my belief forever. It might form the subject-matter of a novel with a good moral.

"I will endeavor to describe the routine of an average day in the home of the Wriedt's.

"At 6 a.m., she and her husband rise, see to the work of the house and prepare breakfast. Breakfast about 8 or 8.30. Mrs. Wriedt clears away the table and proceeds to do the rooms. A telephone bell rings. Perhaps Mr. Wriedt is able to answer it, more likely he has gone out to do the shopping.

"Is that Mrs. Wriedt?"

"Yes."

"Can you give me a sitting?"

"I am sorry to say I am not able to see anyone for ten days."

"Can you not see me for half-an-hour?"

"No, madam."

"What do you charge for a sitting?"

"One dollar."

"Well, I guess a really good sitting is worth one dollar!" Then Mrs. Wriedt goes upstairs to her rooms. Knock at the front door.

"Can I see Mrs. Wriedt?"

"No, sir, I am Mrs. Wriedt, and I am full of engagements for ten days." After some attempt at persuasion this visitor departs. The rooms being finished, say by 10:30, Mrs. Wriedt assures herself that her husband is in the house, and then comes to me: "Admiral, I think now we can have a sitting, and we will have another, if you wish, this evening." We sit, say for forty-five minutes. Soon after, she prepares the dinner, lays the table and answers, perhaps, two or three telephone calls, sometimes these calls are requests for sittings, but not infrequently chats with friends who are in trouble, and sure of the immediate sympathy of the psychic. Dinner at twelve or soon after.

"At half-past one, after the table is cleared, Mrs. Wriedt attires herself for the afternoon. At a quarter to two or two o'clock a party is let in for a seance, promised days before, and remains an hour or an hour and a half. During this time two or three people are admitted into the drawing-room by Mr. Wriedt to wait their turn. Telephone calls answered by Mr. Wriedt at the rate of about one every hour. The first sitters having departed, the second group are taken upstairs (no interval between), and another seance takes place. Mr. Wriedt comes to have a chat, and we both hear distinctly the loud voice of "Dr. Sharp," the control (forty feet off), through the locked door of the séance room. Possibly Mrs. Wriedt is then able to give me a half-hour conversation with my friends in the next state, then she goes down and prepares the tea, her husband having reported to her the telephone calls that came through during the afternoon. Tea takes place about six or a quarter past six. At eight o'clock there is always a seance, arranged for long beforehand, which generally lasts two hours. And so the day's work ends, and the psychic gets to bed about eleven o'clock."

A PUBLIC CIRCLE
THE WRIEDTS HOME, BALDWIN STREET, DETROIT
W. USBORNE MOORE, 1911

"One night I sat in a public circle, when there were twelve persons present besides the psychic and myself. Two young people, brother and sister, sat on my left, they had been invited by Mrs. Wriedt, as they were too poor to give the ordinary fee. "Black Hawk," an Indian spirit, gave a war-whoop when phenomena were going very slowly, which frightened one lady so much that the door had to be opened and water sent for to restore her. Another lady, on hearing the prattling voice of her little child, not long since dead, fell back in her chair, weeping for joy. Her neighbor tried to pull her round by saying: "Try and compose yourself madam, or you will destroy conditions for other sitters." The sobbing then ceased. As the sitters filed out of the room, some of them paid the psychic, who never asks for her fee, the bereaved mother did not give anything. I took the liberty of asking Mrs. Wriedt how much she had received that evening. She told me three and a half dollars. Three people had slunk out of the room without giving a cent, yet all had some friend from the "other side" who came to talk to them, and the seance lasted two hours.

"The failures to obtain phenomena when Mrs. Wriedt is present are about five per cent. If she does too much during the day, Dr. Sharp, her control, does not speak in the evening, and no spirits manifest. Her average takings during a year when she is not ill are seven dollars a day. She has, however, some kind wealthy friends who would never allow her to be in want, so richly do they value the blessings she showers around her. I generally sat alone with Mrs. Wriedt, the strain was great. My physical system was much drawn upon, and I became ill. This was the inevitable payment for extraordinary phenomena. Dr. Sharp would not allow his medium to be depleted, and I, being the only sitter, had to suffer. I did not recover my full, normal self again until I had landed back in England.

"The usual order of proceedings was as follows: I brought bunches of narcissi or some other flowers into the room, and placed them on a small table. Having ascertained that I could hear· the voices in broad light through the trumpet (though with difficulty), we decided to sit in the dark-Mrs. Wriedt on a chair opposite me, and about four feet distant, the table with flowers on my left (generally), and opposite to it a vacant chair, completing a sort of circle, in the center of which was placed a telescopic trumpet. After a few minutes phantoms could be seen about, near us, they appeared first close to the flowers, and returned to them from time to time for strength. I did not once identify a face, though others did, but I knew who was before me by the height, build, and speech of the spirit, for they often spoke with the trumpet while standing. Mrs. Wriedt will sit anywhere her sitters wish, but the above plan was found to answer best. Dr. Sharp, the control, who spoke sometimes through the trumpet and sometimes without, usually manifests early in the seance in a loud, clear voice, and he often comes back at the end of the seance to say "Good-bye," or to explain some doubt which has arisen from the ambiguous utterances of one of the spirits.

"After the phantom phase is over, and Dr. Sharp has finished talking, whispers are heard through the trumpet, and conversation takes place. When I sat alone this used to go on from forty to fifty minutes. The "Good-bye" of Dr. Sharp was the signal for opening the door, if he did not return, we waited five minutes after the last communication, then asked to be told by raps if the seance was over. In the case of no reply we assumed it was no use waiting longer. My notes were made, immediately, in the back drawing-room. I only once attended a public seance, but I often used to sit in my room in the evening, reading and writing, while large seances were going on between 8 and 10 p.m., and heard distinctly the voices, not only of Dr. Sharp, but of other spirits. Curiously enough, no phantoms ever appeared to me in my room, and even my guide was only able to make herself known by knocks. In the description of some of the seances now to be related, names of eminence will appear from time to time.

"Every investigator knows how we are baffled in psychic work by spirits who personate, and I am not prepared to assert that those who came were the distinguished men they purported to be. I prefer to keep an open mind on the subject. I may say, however, that, considering the small number of investigators about, and the anxiety on the part of the inhabitants of the spirit world to make their existence known to the people on the earth plane, I do not see any inherent improbability of even Galileo coming to the seance-room of Mrs. Wriedt to make himself known. Mrs. Wriedt is never in trance. She joins in the conversation with the spirits, and often gives the name and description of a spirit coming before that spirit makes itself known. Her personality evinces itself only in one way: the expressions used by the spirits. My friends spoke pure English, but occasionally their sentences were framed in a way they never used in life. For instance, my guide would reply to a question, "How is so-and-so?" by saying, "Oh! he is getting along all right!" During her life on the earth plane I do not suppose that "Lola" ever made use of such an expression. My mother has been heard to say, "So-and-so is lonesome," a word which certainly was not in her vocabulary when in this life."

SEANCES:
PRIVATE & WITH SITTERS
DETROIT, BY W. USBORNE MOORE
JANUARY 1911

"Arrived at Detroit, and took up my quarters with the Wriedts. There was a séance at 9 p.m. Sitters, Mr. and Mrs. Newton, Mr. H. C. Hodges, and myself. Atmospheric conditions bad. Their two children in spirit life came to Mr. and Mrs. Newton, Mr. Hodges was visited by three spirits who talked in unmistakable Yankee, and I by "Lola," her brother, and the brother of a relative by marriage, who all spoke pure English. "Lola" referred to the seance of the previous evening with Miss Ada Besinnet."

Monday, January 2, 1911, Time, 10.50 to 11.50 a.m.

"First came Dr. Sharp, loud and distinct. He cleared up the identity of one of my visitors the previous night. Then came Sir W. W., who brought Mr. W. E. Gladstone. There were many large, round, illuminated discs and some full-form phantoms. Throughout, I could never identify any spirit by its face, but I could see that there were features. I very nearly recognized the complete face of Mr. Gladstone, his was a tall form, and remained some two minutes.

"After he had disappeared, he spoke through the trumpet. I need not say how surprised I was at this apparition and voice. I had never spoken to Mr. Gladstone during his earth-life, and saw no reason for his coming to me, except perhaps, the fact that one of his distant relatives is a friend of mine, and an ardent inquirer into psychic phenomena, also that I always admired him as a man and a great statesman, and had often thought of him during the recent political struggle. He stopped about twenty minutes, and talked about the conduct and accomplishments of the present Cabinet? I replied: "In my opinion, sir, it is the most brilliant Cabinet that has ever ruled Great Britain, but I wish the Chancellor of the Exchequer would express himself with more moderation, as it would give him more influence." He said: "I do not agree, he must speak out very straight at this juncture. His speech on the Catholic danger was admirable, there must be no religious predominance. We must have Home Rule." He spoke in the highest terms of the present Government, and sent messages to Mr. W. T. Stead.

(Note: Mrs. Wriedt and her husband know nothing of English politics. Mrs. Wriedt had heard a good deal of Mr. Stead.)

"The medium then said: "I hear the name F—. Someone connected with F—is coming. Is it the elder or the younger of the two daughters in spirit life?" A voice: "Good morning, Uncle, I am E—" (surname blurred).

Q.: "Are you E— S—?"

A.: "Yes ..."

Q.: "Are you happy?"

A.: "Very much happier than on earth."

Q.: "Do you often see Lola?"

A.: "Auntie? Oh, yes!"

"There was a talk about her sister in spirit life, and my niece left. (Note the evidence of identity in this case: the acknowledgment by E— S— that she was a daughter of F—, a niece of mine and a niece of Lola-all correct.) Then came a man who could not give me his name, but said he had known me in some foreign place, where I dined with him, we had smoked in the conservatory." He said: "Before you reached home I had passed out. You were ordered to go to this place. You were my guest. I died suddenly."

Q.: "Are you Richard Hodgson?"

A.: "No. It was not in America." (I have not yet identified my visitor, but think I know who it was.)

January 2, 1911. 7.15 to 8.15 p.m.

"With Mrs. Wriedt alone in the dark. After some relatives had come, the psychic heard the names Henry and James (Henry is a brother-in-law of mine). Then a voice came to me through the trumpet, "I am Professor James." We discussed the experiments of Professor Hyslop with Miss Ada Besinnet that were to take place in a few days. After this he said:

"Do you think that Stead would like me to attend his circle? I know his son over here."

I replied: " Yes; I will ask him."

"Thank you. A happy New Year to you." The psychic said, "I hear the name 'Alexander.'" I replied, "I know two Alexanders." A whisper through the tube:

"I am Alexander Usborne, M.'s girl [Lola] brought me here."

We had a little chat about his kindness to me as a boy, and he departed with New Year greetings. Sir Richard Burton then manifested. I said: "You were interested in this subject when in life." Answer, "Yes, I was."

"Question: "It was a pity that your wife destroyed your manuscript."

Answer: "A great pity, but women do queer things at times."

Then followed New Year greetings. After a few minutes the psychic said, "There is a man here who has been shot ... he shot himself. He appears to me to have committed suicide."

A whisper through the trumpet: "George. I was with you in the night." I at once said: "You are George, do you not regret your rash act?"

Then came this remarkable answer:

"No, I do not. I was (emphatically) impelled to do it" (a groan). Admiral, she would not marry me, as I had not enough money, and there was a richer man than I in the background." (a groan).

Question: "What sphere are you in?"

Answer: "The fourth."

Question: "What are your duties?"

Answer: "I help where I can. Admiral, help me with your thoughts. Good-bye."

(This incident took me back twenty years, to a day when an officer under my command shot himself in his cabin. An inquiry was held, and some papers found clearly proving that he had recently received a letter from a girl who had withdrawn her promise to marry him. I do not believe he is in the fourth sphere, or anywhere near it, and, if he maintains his unrepentant attitude, it will be many a long year before he gets there.)

28

"The psychic then said:

"I hear the name of C."

A voice: "I am Mr. C."

Question: "Are you the architect?"

Answer: "Yes."

Question: "I did not know you in your earth life, but I often hear of Mrs. C."

Answer: "Yes, my wife is a wonderful woman-wonderful! but she is now losing her intellect."

(The lady in question is nearly one hundred years of age. Mr. C. was brought by Lola, who spoke at the same time as he did, independently of the trumpet.)

The psychic: "I hear the name of ' Greenleaf. ' I do not know if I have got it quite right." A voice: "Greenfield. I am Mrs. M."

Question: "Which Mrs. M.?—there are two."

The spirit indicated her residence, and said: "I have met you." (There are two Mrs. M.'s—sisters—both are alive. I had met this lady twice. Greenfield is the name of my son-in-law, who is a connection of Mrs. M., and it was evidently used to attract attention. This seems to be a case of an earth spirit travelling during sleep. The time in England was about 2 a.m., January 3. A talk with Lola about family matters closed the seance.)"

Thursday, January 12, 1911. Sitting with Mrs. Wriedt alone, from 2.15 to 3.40 p.m.

"First I tried the trumpet in full light, putting the small end to my left ear and balancing the open end on the back of a chair, Mrs. Wriedt sitting close to me on my right. I heard the voices of Dr. Sharp and Lola quite satisfactorily. This done, we put the lights out and sat in the dark, nothing occurred for half an hour, after which two phantoms were seen close to me, but the faces were not recognizable. The voices commenced with that of my guide, with whom I had a conversation of about twenty minutes, then a sister came who had died at two and a half years of age, and grown up in spirit life. Both alluded to a seance they had attended to meet me at the Jonson's two nights before. Next came an old clergyman at whose school I attended between the ages of six and ten and a half years. He gave the name of Thompson, and followed this up by " John Thompson. " The latter, his son, is alive. Dr. Sharp straightened the matter out thus:

"The man who came was a Dr. Thompson, he was a minister, a doctor of divinity, or something of that sort. You were at his school with his son John Thompson, in order to attract your attention he called out 'John Thompson,' but the latter was not manifesting, it was his father."

January 13, 1911, 2.30 to 4 p.m.

"Sitters were my old friends Mr. and Mrs. Z., their two nieces, and myself. This was a marvelous seance. My friends are old residents of Toledo. They bad long wished to sit with Mrs. Wriedt, but one thing and another had prevented it, and it was destined for me to bring them together. I had sat with them in some other seance-rooms many times, and knew the names of their relatives in spirit life and their guides. Mrs. Wriedt had never seen them, and knew absolutely nothing about them. The three ladies are mediumistic. In a few minutes phantoms began to appear. There were several for the Z. party, one of which was a nun, who is the guide of Mrs. Z. She gave her correct name, "Edna," was fully recognized, and talked some time. Standing in front of us, she pronounced a benediction in Latin, and then repeated it in English, An Indian guide, called "Silvermoon," gave his customary war-whoop in the middle of the seance, then exhibited a large, illuminated disc, and, after a short talk, disappeared.

"Every relation of the Z.'s in spirit life that I ever heard of came and spoke through the trumpet. They correctly mentioned by name several people in earth life, as well as those in spirit life. I was introduced to all. A spirit, name unknown, joined in a song we were singing at the time. The only phenomena for me were an etherealization, which bowed at the name of "father," and my sister Catherine, who said: "I am fifty-six years old as counted in earth life." (On my return home I looked in the family Bible, and found that she was born December 7, 1853.) She also said: "Lola is sitting on that chair beside you." There was a vacant chair between the flowers and myself. This display of spirit power was the more remarkable because the atmospheric conditions were not good, it was thawing."

AN ESTEEMED GUEST:
MEDIUM, ADA BESINNET
RECORDED BY
W. USBORNE MOORE

Sunday, January 22, 1911, 2 to 4 p.m.

"With Mrs. Wriedt. The party consisted of Miss Ada Besinnet (1890-1936), the famous young medium, two of their Detroit friends, and myself. It is a singular fact that the Moores (not connected to Usborne Moore-Ed) and their charge had never met Mrs. Wriedt, and it was reserved for me to bring them together. I sat next to Miss Ada. Her control is an Indian called "Black Cloud," he speaks through her mouth. She was falling into trance by my side when I heard a low voice: "Me no send you to sleep. Me go." The young lady remained awake from this moment to the end of the sitting.

Dr. Sharp came twice, and about ten spirits of relatives and friends of the party satisfactorily identified themselves. My guide came early, and had a talk with Miss Ada, then went to the other end of the circle and identified herself to Mrs. Moore. She and Miss Ada sang together a bar or two of an Indian song. Another spirit sang a few bars of "Home Again" with the young psychic. Silvermoon turned up again (he often functions in Miss Ada's seances), gave his war whoop, talked a little, showed his illuminated disc, and disappeared.

"To me the most interesting feature in this séance was the demonstration of an Indian girl called "Pansy." "Pansy" had been one of the familiar spirits of Maggie Gaule, and, since that psychic's lamentable death in 1910, was more or less free to move about on her own account. Her present occupation seems to be to follow Professor Hyslop in his investigations, and to make fun of him.

"After announcing herself, she said she came with Chief Jim (James Hyslop). She went to Mrs. Moore, and said: "I want to tell you something, but you no tell anyone else-a secret between you and me. Now (turning the voice to us), you people, put your fingers in your ears while I talk to squaw." (Of course, we did nothing of the sort, but listened attentively.)

"Do you know who put ideas into your top-knot to answer Chief Jim?" (A roar of laughter from all.)

"I tell secret to squaw (indignantly).You people no listen, put your fingers in your ears, I tell you."

Then, to Mrs. Moore: "Do you know who put those things into your top-knot to say to Chief Jim? It was Maggie Gaule."

She said several other funny things which delighted the whole party. (James Hyslop had just left Toledo, after an exhaustive examination of Miss Ada Besinnet, and had engaged in several discussions with Mrs. Moore, who often combated his arguments.) Atmospheric conditions perfect."

FEBRUARY SÉANCE
DETROIT, W. USBORNE MOORE
1911

When referring to 'Jonson' it is the powerful materialization medium, Ben Jonson,[8] of Toledo, Ohio (Ed.).

Saturday, February 11, 1911. With Mrs. Wriedt alone, 1.15 to 2.15 p.m.

"Dr. Sharp came with hearty greetings. Alluding to some recent sittings at Toledo, he said: "They have drawn upon you badly, Admiral. It had to be done, the force must be got from someone. I am going to bring an Indian to you. "Then followed some questions and answers on the subject of materialization. (I had been with Jonson the evening before. Jonson was not well, he thought he had lumbago.) An astonishing incident now occurred. "Grayfeather" (who is Jonson's control):

"Chief from across the big pond, I want to say something to you. My medium not fit for anything for one or two weeks. I sorry. I do my best for you, and can do no more. I no kill my medium for anybody. You understand, chief. Joe (Mr. Jonson) he worse than he was yesterday. I impress you to come away. He not know I here, he not know you here. I find out from 'sweet angel' where you come. It is his kidneys, not lumbago, and he been bad ever since he hang that paper on wall. I do no more for you. I sorry."

(Jonson was a paperhanger by trade-Ed)

Q.: "How about Mr. Jonson's heart, Grayfeather?"

---

[8] See: *Dawn of The Awakened Mind,* by Dr. John King, and *The Phenomena of Spirit Materialization,* by N. Riley Heagerty, 2021

A.: "He got no heart, and his kidneys all in trouble. Squaw Jonson sick too."

Mrs. Wriedt said: "I wonder if that is a correct account."

I replied: "I believe it."

Grayfeather: "I never tell lie. If I say I can do nothing, I can do nothing."

I said: "I remember your telling me a perfectly true story two years ago, Grayfeather. Thank you for your communication. I shall write to your medium this afternoon. Tell me, Grayfeather, how was it that my guide was able to pull her hand away from mine the other afternoon?"

Grayfeather: "I help her, and I draw from your legs to keep her on her feet. I draw much from you, if I not draw from you, spirit form will go all to pieces. "

Q.: "Then it is injurious to your medium for a form to dematerialize quickly?"

A.: "They should fall very slowly. Chief, may I come to you across the big pond?"

Q.: "Very glad, Grayfeather, if you will. Thank you very much. Goodbye. I hope to come back in two years."

A.: "I not sure Joe be here then (mournfully). When he go, I go too."

(One remarkable feature in Grayfeather's visit was that his voice direct was very similar to Jonson's control when he speaks through the organism of Jonson at Toledo. At the close of the sitting I wrote to Mr. Jonson, giving him a full account of Grayfeather's warning. I followed this up with a visit on Monday, February 13, p.m., and found him then fully disposed to take his disease seriously. We cancelled all engagements, and I have not seen him since.)

My guide came in for a long chat.

Q.: "Do you know where I was yesterday?"

A.: "Yes."

Q.: "There was one phenomenon at Jonson's?"

A.: "Yes, the trumpet, I said 'Lola.'" (Correct.)

Q.: "Where was I in the evening?"

A.: "At the sweet young girl's." (Correct, Miss Ada's seance.)

Q.: "Who wrote those notes to me?"

A.: "The medium wrote all those, automatic writing."

MRS WRIEDT IN NEW YORK
FEBRUARY, 1911
W. USBORNE MOORE

"It so happened that Mrs. Wriedt came to New York on a visit to friends on February 23. The lady of the house most kindly accorded me permission to have a sitting with the psychic in private on February 24. It took place in the morning, between 10.5 and 11.15. Atmospheric conditions perfect.

"My guide had, by this time, become very proficient in using the direct voice, with and without the assistance of the trumpet, but I hardly expected her to show the amount of power that was exhibited on this occasion. After a short interval-say five minutes-she made herself known through the trumpet, and spoke for fifty minutes on certain important private matters. I asked her what I had been doing the previous evening, and she gave me an exact description of how my time had been employed, beginning in this way: "At 8.20 we called at a house in—then followed a little story showing a fair general acquaintance with the inmates of the house, and evincing an accurate knowledge of their aims in life. It left me in no doubt as to her presence with me on that visit. Dr. Sharp then came for five minutes, and gave me a hearty send-off, in his usual genial manner. I sailed the next morning for England."

No Psychic has Ever Brought me so Near to the Spirit Life

"In closing my experiences with Mrs. Wriedt in America, I must add a few comments. I am without any receptive mediumistic gifts, and claim no more natural powers of hearing and seeing than the average man of my age. I am conscious that, during the sittings I had with this gifted psychic, I may have missed much which younger men, or those even slightly endowed with clairaudient and clairvoyant powers, would have heard and seen. Often it happened that others heard messages which I did not, and saw full forms and faces that I was unable to distinguish. It must not be supposed, therefore, that I have been able to give a wholly fair estimate of what usually takes place in her presence. No psychic has ever brought me so near to the spirit life. It is to Mrs. Wriedt that I owe the absolute knowledge of the near proximity of my friends who have passed over, and I feel greatly indebted to her for making it so easy for me to obtain that knowledge.

"It is a possession of priceless value, it outwears all time, and places the fortunate man who has it in a position of certainty that death has no sting and the grave no victory, that what is, is right, that all things work together for good, and that our brief span on earth, acquiring our individuality, is but the introduction to a higher life of greater possibilities of usefulness and expansion.

"Mrs. Wriedt believes there are no such entities as evil spirits. Not one has ever entered her room. It took me some time to explain to her that their name is legion, and that it is owing to the vigilance of Dr. Sharp they are warned off her premises. The utterances of spirits in her presence exhibit all the human emotions except anger. Moderation, tact, and loving-kindness are the watchwords. She is indeed blessed in having been the passive instrument of consolation and rest to hundreds, and hope to thousands who have come within the influence of her psychic power. It is to be hoped that her frail life may be preserved for many years. I am most grateful also to her hearty control, Dr. Sharp, whom I look upon now as an old friend."

ATTEMPT TO DISCREDIT
MRS. WRIEDT

I thought I would add this little item from Nandor Fodor's *Encyclopedia of Psychic Science* made by these medium hating narcissists. They of course failed to discredit this giant of psychic fame and only made themselves out to be more imbecilic than they already were (Ed.).

"An attempt to throw discredit on Mrs. Wriedt's phenomena was made in Christiania in August 1912, by Professor Birkenhead and State Chemist L. Schmelck. They averred that the noises in the trumpet were caused by lycopodium, a mildly inflammable powder used by druggists to coat pills. The facts, however, were very thin, other chemists held the report up to ridicule, moreover it became known that Prof. Birkenhead is extremely deaf and could not judge voices at all."

3

WITNESSES TO WONDERS

They Came, They Saw, They Heard, They Documented

~

"Nothing is too Wonderful to be True."

~ MICHAEL FARADAY

The following are the finest collection of eyewitness accounts involving the direct voice/trumpet séances of Etta Wriedt. My goal was to have all the testimonies-edited-in one book and here they are. All of the great mediums of the past should have been so lucky to have such intelligent, rational individuals of integrity document their experiences. Let their testimonies live on forever and may future generations one day discover these colossal events that proved beyond a shadow of a doubt the positivity of life after death and spirit communication. Victorian Spiritualism at its best.

SIR ARTHUR CONAN DOYLE
THE NEW REVELATION
1918

"Direct Voice phenomena are different from mere clairvoyance and trance-speaking in that the sounds do not appear to come from the medium but externalize themselves often to a distance of several yards, continue to sound when the mouth is filled with water, and even break into two or three voices simultaneously. On these occasions an aluminum trumpet is used to magnify the voice, and also, as some suppose to form a small dark chamber in which the actual vocal cords used by the spirit can become materialized. It is an interesting fact, and one which has caused much misgiving to those whose experience is limited, that the first sounds usually resemble the voice of the medium. This very soon passes away and the voice either becomes neutral or may closely resemble that of the deceased. It is possible that the reason of this phenomenon is that the ectoplasm from which the phenomena are produced is drawn from him or her, and carries with it some of his or her peculiarities until such time as the outside force gains command. It is well that the skeptic should be patient and await developments, for I have known an ignorant and self-opinionated investigator take for granted that there was fraud through noting the resemblance of voices, and then wreck the whole séance by foolish horseplay, whereas had he waited his doubts would soon have been resolved.

"The author has had the experience with Mrs. Wriedt of hearing the Direct Voice, accompanied by raps on the trumpet, in broad daylight, with the medium seated some yards away. This disposes of the idea that the medium in the dark can change her position. It is not uncommon to have two or three spirit voices speaking or singing at the same moment, which is in turn fatal to the theory of ventriloquism. The trumpet, too, which is often decorated with a small spot of luminous paint, may be seen darting about far out of reach of the medium's hands. On one occasion at the house of Mr. Dennis Bradley, the author saw the illuminated trumpet whirling round and tapping on the ceiling as a moth might have done. The medium (Valiantine)[9] was afterwards asked

---

[9] George Valiantine (1874-1947), American direct voice medium from Williamsport, Pennsylvania. See: H. Dennis Bradley's, *Towards The Stars*, 1924, *Wisdom of The Gods*, 1925, T. Werner Laurie, London.

to stand upon his chair, and it was found that with the trumpet in his extended arm he was unable to touch the ceiling. This was witnessed by a circle of eight.

"Mrs. Wriedt was born in Detroit (Wrong, Oswego, NY-Ed) some fifty years ago, and is perhaps better known in England than any American medium. The reality of her powers may best be judged by a short description of results. On the occasion of a visit to the author's house in the country she sat with the author, his wife, and his secretary, in a well-lighted room. A hymn was sung, and before the first verse was ended a fifth voice of excellent quality joined in and continued to the end. All three observers were ready to depose that Mrs. Wriedt herself was singing all the time. At the evening sitting a succession of friends came through with every possible, sign of their identity. One sitter was approached by her father, recently dead, who began by the hard, dry cough which had appeared in his last illness. He discussed the question of some legacy in a perfectly rational manner. A friend of the author's, a rather irritable Anglo-Indian, manifested, so far as a voice could do so, reproducing exactly the fashion of speech, giving the name, and alluding to facts of his lifetime. Another sitter had a visit from one who claimed to be his grand aunt. The relationship was denied, but on inquiry at home it was found that he had actually had an aunt of that name who died in his childhood. Telepathy has to be strained very far to cover such cases."

This next section was written by James Robertson, and without question his book, mentioned in the footnote, is one of the best I have ever read and a must read for all enthusiasts of this marvelous subject. His words below concerning Etta Wriedt are a shining gem of Spiritualism and written with heart, soul, and erudition, a true classic (Ed.).

JAMES ROBERTSON:
THE OPEN DOOR TO
THE UNSEEN UNIVERSE
NOVEMBER 11, 1912

W. Usborne Moore

"My friend Mr. James Robertson, of Glasgow, is a bicycle manufacturer. He is seventy years of age, a Spiritualist of some thirty-five years' standing, and author of *Spiritualism The Open Door to the Unseen Universe*,[10] Although he leaves it to my discretion to "cut and carve" as much as I like, I prefer to leave his narrative just as he wrote it. It reveals the man better than anything I can say of him. His letter is appended: 5 Granby Terrace, Glasgow, W. November 11, 1912."

Dear Usborne Moore:
"I now send you some pages I have penned, and, though they may lack the direct point which your own articles have conveyed, still I hope you will be able to make some use of them. I cannot say that I am at all pleased with what is sent, and had some thoughts of beginning again, but have resolved to let them go as they are. The beginning you will think perhaps out of place. One of my daughters to whom I handed the pages for perusal said: "Cut all that out," but I will leave you to cut and carve as much as you like, and if you should think of sending them back to me with any hints I will do what you may desire. With all kind regards and appreciation of your grand work."
Yours most sincerely,
James Robertson

---

[10] *Spiritualism: The Open Door to The Unseen Universe*, by James Robertson, L. N. Fowler & Co., London, 1908. Being Thirty Years of Personal Observation and Experience concerning Intercourse between the Material and Spiritual Worlds, offers a unique insider's perspective on the growing Spiritualist movement in Scotland and England from the late Victorian era through to the dawn of the 20th century. Originally published in The Two Worlds magazine over the course of 30 years, Scottish author James Robertson and editor J.J. Morse compiled these essays into a single volume in 1908. Robertson describes in detail the activities and meetings of the still-extant Glasgow Association of Spiritualists. He also thoughtfully discusses topics such as the religion and literature of Spiritualism, Spiritualist organizations and periodicals of the era, and phenomena such as automatic writing and spirit photography.

"Carlyle has said:"

"Men have lost their faith in the Invisible, and believe and hope and work only in the Visible." The belief in another world, whose inhabitants could take cognizance of this sphere, has been of import to us. Of course, we had traditions, which we thought we believed in, but no feeling of certainty came into our lives. The wisest and best of men, with the largest culture of the intellect, found nothing in their investigations of external nature which gave the slightest hint of this invisible world of which ancient books had somewhat feebly spoken. That the world could become possessed of such new phenomena, a new power and knowledge that could relate us to an invisible world, was thought to be the rudest conception that could be offered. Neither the men of accomplished minds nor the custodians of religious verities would admit for a long time that nature had such possibilities to unfold. It has to be admitted that this new phenomena, [sic] which claimed to relate us to this unseen universe, did not show their best face at first. It seemed crude and rude that a revelation of such transcendent importance as the opening of the gates of that other world should be ushered in by noises, which naturally clashed with our prepossessions regarding that hidden realm.

"It was an appeal only to our external senses. But, like every new thing, it gradually presented to the world a more varied program, the same power which caused the rappings claimed to move the pen and lips of those who first paid attention to the matter, and soon there were great numbers who spoke out messages that bore evidence of being prompted by those whom we had talked about as dead. A light began to shine in the darkness, scientific and scholarly minds were attracted to the subject, and found that the messages poured out were neither unintelligible nor obscure, but bore the stamp of reason, of wisdom, and were in accord with the principles of nature. How the light spread at first over the continent of Europe, and eventually found a footing in England, it is not my province to dwell upon. That such men as D. D. Home[11] raised the temperature of many thinking minds is undoubted.

[11] Daniel Dunglas Home (1833-1886), One of the most famous and powerful mediums in the history of Modern Spiritualism. See Home's two books: *Incidents of My Life*, 1862, and a second series in 1872, and *Lights and Shadows of Spiritualism*, 1873; Madame Home's *D. D. Home, His Life and Mission*, 1877, and *The Gift of D. D. Home*, 1890; Lord Adare's *Experiences in Spiritualism with D. D. Home*, 1869

The phenomena which transpired in his presence dissipated much of the materialism which abounded, and gave an elevation of soul to many who were made to feel that religion might be a tangible thing after all. That such men as Crookes, Wallace, and Robert Chambers were attracted to this man evidences that there was a portent of noble quality running through him. Thackeray was brave enough to admit into the columns of the *Cornhill* magazine (then in its palmy days) an article which described the phenomena that transpired in Home's presence. Society invariably shows small favors to its guides and teachers, and so Home, with all his striking gifts, which brought consolation to weary hearts, had to run the gauntlet of fierce opposition. Many a poisoned arrow was aimed at him, but he left behind a record which is unassailable.

"It is quite thirty-six years since I was drawn into contact with this modern spiritual movement, at a time when I utterly disbelieved in the possibility of any light on the subject of a future life being possible. It is said that to become thoroughly acquainted with a truth we must first have disputed it. I held the idea in 'such contempt that I could not calmly listen to its claims, and yet, when I did open my mind and viewed the facts, these facts beat me, and I have never had cause to retrace my steps. It was illuminating, throwing a light for me on every realm of thought. Vague yearnings were satisfied, dreamy fancies became realities. It became a fountain whose waters refreshed with gladness my whole being. It was crude phenomena, which the world would laugh at, that brought the conviction that unseen beings could act on matter, that they could see us, read our minds, and reveal an intelligence outside the knowledge of the sitters. It has been my privilege to come into close contact with nearly all the phenomenal mediums, whose powers make evident that they are but the servants of those who are wiser than themselves.

"Light has been shed through every form of mediumship. I have looked at faces I had known on earth, I have heard descriptions given by clairvoyants which were photographic of the person described, I have had messages hundreds of times which could only bear one interpretation—that is, they were the thoughts of those we called dead. I knew intimately for years the three brothers Duguid,[12] who were most

---

[12] David Duguid (1832-1907), Glasgow, non-professional medium, chiefly famous for his automatic writing and drawing mediumship; brothers Robert and Alexander who were psychic but far eclipsed by their brothers fame. See: *Hafed: Prince of Persia*, 1876.

plastic in the hands of the spirit operators. I became intimate with their inspirers and helpers, and I have the conviction that these spirit workers were all they claimed to be—simple-minded Indians, or philosophers, or painters such as Jan Steen and Euisdael. This other world has a mission to bring home to earth-dwellers that immortality is a natural fact, and that the real salvation of the world will be brought about when humanity realizes its truth. I have had close acquaintanceship with the workers whose mental phenomena have produced a literature which cannot die away into insignificance and oblivion, for the writings of Davis and Tuttle are a perennial well from which the most useful knowledge comes forth.

"Years of friendly converse with the inspirers of Mr. J. J. Morse[13] and Mr. E. W. Wallis[14] have built up a conviction which nothing can destroy. It has been in my own home—perhaps sitting with my own family—that my inmost heart has been reached, and all doubt of the loving friendship of spirit people has been dissipated forever. I thought after thirty-five years' close observation that I had been brought as close to the spirit people as ever I would likely get, but in this I have been mistaken. I had clear memories of Lottie Fowler's[15] wonderful mediumship, which perhaps was the most striking of my experience. A fragile woman, yet one who forced conviction on you, your whole

---

[13] J. J. Morse (1848-1919)
One of the most prominent trance speakers of the nineteenth century, designated the "Bishop of Spiritualism" by Spiritualist journalist W. T. Stead.

[14] E. W. Wallis (1848-1914)
British trance medium, inspirational speaker, healer, lecturer, and author. "Lightheart," the spirit of a South American Indian, claimed responsibility for his mediumistic development. "Standard Bearer," "Leader," and "Tom Joyce" were others of his well-known controls.

Assisted by his wife, also a notable psychic, Wallis did propaganda work for many decades. He assisted Emma H. Britten in starting the journal *The Two Worlds* in Manchester, which he edited until 1899. In that year he came to London and became editor of *Light*, a position he held until his death.

[15] Lottie Fowler (1836-1899)
Real name: Charlotte Connolly—American clairvoyant, medical diagnose, the medium who introduced Stainton Moses to Spiritualism in April 1872, on her visit to England. Fritz's *Where are the Dead*, London, 1873, Hellenbach's *Eine Philosophie des Gesunden Menschenverstandes* and Forence Marryat's two books *There is no Death*, London, 1892, and *The Spirit World*, London, 1894, contain interesting narratives of her powers.

life and its circumstances being opened out. I have always thought of her as being the high-water mark of mediumistic development. It was a vision which could not be disputed, but it was fitful and erratic, becoming cloudy at intervals, the woman herself giving little idea of spiritual development. She was a machine through which spirit people found they could carry conviction of their presence and powder. I have met with many who, through her gifts, have been brought from the depths of their grief to participate in a pure joy. I had thought, as I have said, till the autumn of 1911 that the channel of communication had been opened as wide as it would ever be in my day.

"I had read Admiral Moore's clear-cut descriptions in *Light*[16] of his experiences with Mrs. Wriedt of Detroit, and had perhaps the feeling that the statements made were colored, or that America gave conditions which were not available in this country. This doubt, however, had soon to be dissipated. My friend, Councillor Appleyard, of Sheffield, wrote me that he had Mrs. Wriedt as a guest staying with him, that he proposed bringing her north on a holiday jaunt, and that she would be pleased to give me a sitting, with liberty to invite such friends as I desired. I spent the evening of her arrival at her hotel, and the next morning, with Mr. and Mrs. Appleyard, we went on an excursion to Loch Long and Loch Lomond. I had a whole day's converse with her, and found her clear, simple, and true, glittering with no luster but that of common sense. At night there were gathered together in my library the friends and relatives whom I had invited—a company of fifteen persons in all.

"The place in which we sat had oft-times been used for such gatherings, while the group of persons assembled had all seen something of the subject except one man, a minister of the Church of Scotland. I had met this gentleman on board a steamer while on a trip to the Canary Islands a short time before, I had given him a promise that if, at any time, I had any satisfactory evidence to offer which would substantiate the truth of what we had spoken so much about, I would invite him to be present.

"We sat in the darkness, the trumpet having before this been brought out of its case and handed round for inspection, being afterwards set on the floor in the middle of the room. I was not anxious for any tests of spirit identity personally, my wish being that the others who needed it

---

[16] *Light: A Journal of Psychical, Occult, and Mystical Research* was a British weekly periodical created by *The Spiritualist Alliance* and published since 1881. It was one of the most famous of all Spiritualist publications.

more might get the full assurance that had been mine for so many years. My desires, however, did not rule. We had been conversing together for only a few minutes when a loud and clear voice was heard speaking, Mrs. Wriedt informing us that this was Dr. Sharp, whose work it was to manage matters from his side of life, I heard voices speaking, faintly, close to me but could not well make out what was said.

"Did I not know Harry Smith?" I was asked by the Doctor.

"Yes," I said, and then Harry related his story, which was not of any deep import to me beyond the great fact it demonstrated that here was one I had known on earth who could still interest himself in me. Harry Smith was a mechanic who had been in my employment for many years. Of course he knew of my devotion to spiritualism, and had heard me speak at our hall. Not only had become, but he had brought with him several other old servants who were determined to speak, and would only resign the trumpet when they were fully recognized. I confess that, while this talk was going on, I was anxious would end, I felt I was monopolizing the power, while the stories of these old mechanics were not of the first importance to me. There they were, however, and left quite happy when I had admitted the truth of some trifling incident they brought to my memory.

"A most interesting feature in all this was the part played by Dr. Sharp. You felt here was a strong, robust nature who was guiding a team, pulling up this one and letting some other go in front, determined that those he let come to the front should be understood, while Mrs. Wriedt came in now and again with a word to straighten out matters when they were apt to get confused. The form of mediumship I was now witnessing was quite new to me. I felt I was being brought closer than ever before to the dead, there was a sense of face-to-face conversation, a steady, continuous stream of speech, not fugitive and streaky, but robust and direct. The unseen friends seemed determined that I should be saturated with evidence, whether I desired it or not.

"My son-in-law, who was accidentally killed in Italy some years ago, came and revealed a personality about which there could be no mistake. Evidently Dr. Sharp had no trouble in teaching him how to use the trumpet, he was a man of quick intelligence, scientific to the fingertips. He spoke of the past so clearly, and of the present position of his wife and children, naming them without hesitation, and showing that he had the most complete knowledge of things as they were. It was among the finest bits of evidence I ever had that the veil which separated human hearts was a very thin one. Some things which were not detailed, but suggested, carried as much to my mind as his other narrative, the subtle hints were a revelation of character which could scarcely have been more complete. That the members of the family were deeply moved is only a prosaic expression, there was a stirring up of the whole nature, a confidence which no time can weaken, a knowledge which will warm life, and a light borne in which is real sunshine.

"My dear old mother, who in the earth life had so many regrets that I had drifted to what she called " unbelief, " came and expressed her gladness that I had followed the light that had come. Of her presence in our midst I had oft-times been made familiar, but here she was again, if not in the body at least in the heart. She spoke to my girls, who were present, as only she and no other would speak, calling them by the pet names she used while on earth, and which had been forgotten, made reference by name to other members of the family, and revealed an identity about which there could be no mistake. The voice of my mother was the voice I was familiar with, the same broad Doric speech, as if she had never gone from us.

"The Scotch idioms were never departed from for a moment, if we did not see her in the habit in which she lived, we, at least, felt she was unchanged in manner, the girls present were still children to her, and her memory of the earth life and its people quite keen. She spoke to me as if we had but parted yesterday, called me "Jeems" as she had always done while in the body, and as she had often done since when influencing other mediums to speak to me. Here, it was speaking direct as it were without using another's voice. Mrs. Wriedt could not by any possibility have given a replica of the Scotch tones I heard, for while my mother was conversing with my daughters the medium was talking in her usual Yankee tones.

"It was not my mother alone who spoke in true Scotch, each one of the spirit visitors who had been natives communication with his two sons, who had been drowned in the Atlantic, in the purest Scotch, and marvelous was the knowledge they seemed to have of their father's going-out and coming-in in his daily life. A clever imitator could not keep up the Scottish dialect beyond a few words, he could not deceive a native who had been used to our lowland Scotch. Dr. Sharp, the controlling intelligence, who claimed to have been a native of Glasgow, used many Scotch words, quite like one of ourselves, but he did not keep this up for long. Once, when he asked us to sing together an old Scotch song, which he named with a true accent, I asked him where he could have heard it, he at once said, "I learned it at my mother's knee."

"All of this conversing with the so-called dead, however regarded by those who have not come in touch with spiritual phenomena, had no relation to miracle, magic, or monkish legends, but was a plain, natural fact, proving that the world of spirit and the world of matter were no longer twain, but locked into one. As Milton said long ago: "Man is one aspect of Him," and here was the evidence. Perhaps as striking as my own experiences were those of the clergyman who had not come close to the subject before. He had at one time had a charge in Canada, and quite a number of his old parishioners came and spoke to him. It was amusing to hear some of the quaint names, which the minister recognized at once, and the incidents which were recalled to his mind. " I don't remember that, Jerry," the minister would say, but Jerry would go on bringing out something more which had to be admitted. Incidents of his Canadian career were told out and accepted without difficulty. A brother also came to him and spoke about all the members of his family. The minister evidently felt that what we were participating in was the common daily food with which spiritualists were regaled at their gatherings. He had no idea of the patient efforts by which many had drawn together the accumulated bits that had brought conviction. It is not often that anyone at once has the evidence of the unseen world brought home conclusively.

"But something of more importance was to follow. A personality of more importance now came upon the scene, a voice unlike all the others which preceded it—that of Andrew Jackson Davis.[17] The great seer had been very close to me for years, while in the body our correspondence was frequent, and he unburdened himself to me about many things which were unknown to the world. After his death he gave me a message to send to his wife through the mediumship of Miss McCreadie, and asked her to send me the skullcap he wore at home, which his wife, accepting the message as valid, at once did, so that it will be seen that there was a link formed between Davis and myself which would naturally bring him into my surroundings. It was not to

[17] Andrew Jackson Davis (August 11, 1826 – January 13, 1910) was an American Spiritualist, born in Blooming Grove, New York. Davis had little education. In 1843 he heard lectures in Poughkeepsie on animal magnetism, the precursor of hypnotism, and came to perceive himself as having remarkable clairvoyant powers. In the following year he received, he said, spiritual messages telling him of his life work. He described himself as "the Poughkeepsie Seer. He wrote *The Great Harmonia* between 1850-1861, *The Penetralia*, 1856, *The Magic Staff*, 1857.

me, however, so much as the clergyman to whom Davis spoke. He had evidently read his mind, and seen the wavering between the wish to believe and the ability to do so.

"With a lofty eloquence and clear, calm enthusiasm for truth, he gave a reading of the inner side of his nature, and urged him to follow the light that had come to him, at whatever cost. It was a magnificent piece of rhetoric, burning with the loftiest ideals. It was purely spiritual, the mundane being cast aside. Scarcely ever before had I listened to an address from the spirit side that conveyed so much, compressed into such a short space. It did not go beyond the senses' comprehension, there was nothing suffuse, but a simple sublimity that touched all. The seer who had given himself to the discovery of truth seemed bent on its diffusion. The minister said but little, he recognized that the person who spoke had read his heart, knew all his doubts and fears, and how his mind had been swaying to and from. When he had returned to his parish he at once wrote me that, while he never doubted the reality of the unseen world, what had been given at that seance was most extraordinary.

"It is cheering and assuring," he continued, "that the communication can be so clearly established."

"Andrew Jackson Davis's address to me will remain vivid and impressive, and I hope inspiring, during my earth life. That some chord was struck and kept vibrating is evidenced from the fact that, a few weeks afterwards, I was surprised to hear from him that he had resigned his charge, where he was loved and respected. Davis had evidently given his mental struggles some power to come to a decision as to his attitude towards truth as it was now presented to him. I do not know that what he wrote me revealed to the full the influence the seance had upon him. He wrote: "Lest you attach any blame to yourself (I had advised him to hold on to his work, as, situated as he was, his sympathy and tenderness would be an influence for good, more perhaps than in the open field), I hasten to say that, perhaps for twelve years, I have thought as I now think, and have fought against the thought, compromised, and did as well as I could. I will confess, however, that Mr. Davis's words at the seance thrilled me. I need not add more on this point, but return to other incidents of the seance. Dr. Sharp explained the difficulty he had in teaching the crowd who were around us how to form the vocal chord, so that we might hear the voices clearly. One old friend of mine, who was present, is a lady who has waded through a sea of troubles, many of a very tragic nature, yet ever feeling strengthened through the blessed light of spirit communion. There are some persons who find no difficulty in their quest for light.

"I have met with those who, I was apt to think, were credulous, so readily did spiritual communications reach them, but I have learned to recognize that there is a receptivity in the nature of some which is not in others, that, while many have to wait outside the gates for long before conviction comes, there are others who in a moment recognize the reality of the spirit's presence. To this lady there came messages which touched and reached her inmost heart. All flowed to her so naturally, the messages from husband and family gone on. There was only one conviction that could be borne in—that a door was actually open through which the inhabitants of another world came and gave us some glimpses of their continued affection, and of their active, earnest, natural life. I know that such gatherings as I am seeking to chronicle are rare. With us there was the most complete harmony—each was calm and confiding. With one accord and mind we sat in a room which had been oft-times magnetized with the spirits' presence, so that what might be called perfect conditions prevailed. If what transpired among us, the many bits of spirit identity, could only have been realized by the outside world, then the great question had been conclusively settled. Doubt could no more prevail, gloom and darkness would disappear, for we had the certainty that our dead (so-called) were alive.

"I have not given a garbled description of what transpired, yet I have left untold many bits of deep interest which concerned the several sitters, all of whom had some conclusive evidence. Wonderful was the playing on an unseen cornet and the melodious voices which sang at intervals. We sat for over two hours amid this ameliorating and uplifting influence.

"How much more of evidence regarding a future state must needs be given before the minds of humanity see? Conan Doyle had said: "We were so conservative in our temperament that it took three generations before a proved fact, if it was a novel one, could enter into the minds of the people, with the view of its being incorporated into the daily life. Three generations have now gone since the advent of modern spiritualism, so that the ripened period is at hand when across the doorway the greetings of the unseen will be gratefully accepted."

"Mrs. Wriedt, unlike others who have carried the torch of truth, makes no claim to be a superior person, but only an instrument who helps to reveal, in measure, the possibilities that belong to our human nature. It was admirable to see the calm, unaffected manner with which she sat through the proceedings—a spectator seemingly outside it all, nothing seemingly abnormal. There was no show of vanity or conceit, only *a sense of gladness that so much consolation had come to those who had gathered* together. All the marvels I had witnessed before were a prophecy of what had now come before me, and I saw in the future time a still further evolution of spiritual gifts springing forth which would remove the last tinge of doubt regarding an after-death state.

"Never before was I so deeply affected by the great possibilities the future had in store. I saw the crust of prejudice being broken through and a new and brighter color given to human life through the certainty that death does not put an end to the cooperation which had existed. Other voices will be heard which will win their way to the world's recognition that there has been found a pathway to another world. However doubtful be the welcome they may receive now, there is no cause for fear, they will stay in our midst till recognition has come. And it is certain that, even as the evidence has become more clear, and science has begun to give attention to the subject in our day, the doorway will open wider all the time. The volume of well-attested facts which Admiral Moore has brought together cannot be sneered at nor ignored, they are in line with what Crookes and Wallace had previously attested, and in harmony with the natural world in which we live.

"During the summer of 1912 I have been privileged to be present at several other gatherings at which Mrs. Wriedt has been present. At all of these there have been similar revealments of the presence of my dead friends, and messages given in languages of which the medium could have no knowledge. I have realized more fully than ever that we do not need to wait till death before we can come into touch with the spirit world. As Gerald Massey[18] has said: " Instead of the other world remaining dim and helplessly afar off—a possibility to some, a doubt to others, a perplexity to many, and an abstraction to most—it will be made a living verity, visible to many, audible to more, present with and operant through all."

---

[18] Gerald Massey (29 May 1828 – 29 October 1907) was an English poet and writer on Spiritualism and Ancient Egypt.

ERNEST A. S. HAYWARD
Psychic Experiences Throughout The World
London, 1939

Our First Experience-sittings with Mrs. Etta Wriedt

"Prior to July 1922, we were not only skeptical of, but absolutely opposed to, the subject of Spiritualism, and, apart from reading occasional newspaper articles, usually of a depreciatory nature, we had but slight knowledge of and no desire to investigate it.

"We had lost our son Brenton in Flanders in 1915, and our daughter Cecily had passed away in 1919 after a long and painful illness brought about by her war work in the trying climate of Malta.[19] Their loss had left an aching void in our hearts, as we had been a devoted family, but we felt that it would not be right (even if it were possible) to bring them back, as we thought, to earth conditions especially after the suffering they had undergone prior to their passing. We little knew then the joy it gives them to return to inspire and help those near and dear to them. As it was, we could not obtain any comfort from the teachings of the orthodox Churches, (Ed-Of course not) holding out as they do a vague hope of reunions at some immeasurably distant future, so we became interested in Theosophy, which satisfied our desire for knowledge of a future life.

"At that time we were living in London, as I was then an assistant director at the Admiralty, and one afternoon, at the invitation of the widow of an army officer who had known us and our children in Malta, my wife attended a lecture at the *Theosophical Club* at Lancaster Gate. At the close, our friend pointed out a lady in the audience whom she said was a Spiritualist, and asked my wife is she would like to meet her. She replied, "You know I don't want to have anything to do with Spiritualism." However, after some persuasion she agreed to the introduction.

"During the course of the ensuing conversation, this lady, who was Irish-Miss Thompson by name-asked her if she was interested in Spiritualism. My wife gave an emphatic "No!" Later, Miss Thompson asked her if she would like to look at some psychic photographs. Not wishing to appear rude, my wife consented. Those that were shown her

---

[19] Malta is an island in an archipelago in the central Mediterranean between Sicily and the North African coast.

did not specially impress her, until Miss Thompson handed her one which she said had been taken by a Mrs. Deane[20] three months before, and explained that she had sent it round to her friends in England and Ireland, so that the "extra" upon it might, if possible, be recognized. It appeared that she had a lost a very dear brother and had sat several times with Mrs. Deane in the hope that she might obtain his psychic photograph, but on every occasion the face of a stranger had appeared. As soon as my wife looked at it she gasped, in her intense amazement, at recognizing it as a picture of our daughter-not a copy of an existing one, but indubitably her likeness. She said, "Why, this is a picture of my daughter!" Miss Thompson asked, "Are you sure?" I replied. "Certainly. A mother cannot mistake the likeness of her own daughter." The ectoplasm was shaped like an Irish harp, and in the center, where the strings would have been, was Cecily's beautiful face. Our daughter had always been most artistic, and it was just such a thing as she would have done, as a compliment to Miss Thompson's nationality.

"My wife at once thought that if our daughter could show herself on a stranger's photograph three months before she met her, there must be something in Spiritualism, and there must be some way in which she could get in touch with her.

"Thereupon she became as eager to learn all she could, as hitherto she had been averse to the idea, and asked Miss Thompson how she could set about doing so. The latter replied that there was in London the famous "direct voice" medium, Mrs. Etta Wriedt, of Detroit, U.S.A., with whom she had sat on several occasions, but she explained that it was hopeless to expect to get a sitting, as she was usually almost fully booked up before her arrival.

"My wife was very persistent, and eventually to silence her opportunity, Miss Thompson agreed to write and ask her if she would give a sitting for a friend, mentioning no name.

"At my wife's request, Miss Thompson gave her the photograph to show to me, and I immediately recognized the likeness, although completely at a loss to account for it.

"A few days later, much to Miss Thompson's surprise, Mrs. Wriedt replied acquiescing, and fixed a date for the sitting. As my wife did not know the first thing about a séance, and was accordingly somewhat nervous, she invited Miss Thompson to accompany her, who accepted with much pleasure.

---

[20] Mrs. Ada Emma Deane: Well-known English spirit photographer.

"At the time fixed, they both went to where Mrs. Wriedt was staying. No formal introduction was made on arrival. They were shown up to the séance room, which Mrs. Wriedt invited my wife to examine thoroughly, to satisfy herself that there was no hidden apparatus in it, or in the very limited amount of furniture, for fraudulent production of the voices. After doing this, they sat down, and a collapsible trumpet, which was used by the communicating spirits as a kind of megaphone for amplifying the voices, was placed on the floor midway between them and out of reach of the medium and sitters alike.

Mrs. Wriedt then extinguished the electric light, and my wife's first séance began. "There was a small table near where she sat, and in the darkness, unknown to the medium, she placed on it our daughter's psychic photograph which she had brought with her, together with a bunch of violets, which she had bought on the way. Mrs. Wriedt began by describing, clairvoyantly, a young girl turning over sheets of music and standing near a piano, and from the description my wife recognized that it was Cecily, who had been very musical and the possessor of a very beautiful voice, which she had used in concert parties which had been organized in Malta for the entertaining of the sick and wounded soldiers at the hospitals during the war.

"Mrs. Wriedt did not go into trance, and, very soon, a man's loud voice was heard, announcing that he was Dr. Sharp, the principal control. He greeted my wife by name, and described some of the spirits who were waiting to speak to her. She then heard a voice saying, "*dov'e mia madre?*" (Italian for "Where is my mother?") Mrs. Wriedt asked what the voice was saying, as she knew no foreign languages. My wife recognized at once that it was Cecily who was speaking, as she called out these words when she entered our official residence in Malta. It was very large, having been one of the palaces of the Knights Commanders of the Galleys in the time of the Knights of St. John, and, by so calling out, she saved herself the trouble of searching for her. She then spoke, giving many details to prove her identity. She finished by saying, "Mother, how did you like my psychic photograph? That was t*he only way* I could reach you," and thanked her for bringing the violets. Cecily had known how skeptical my wife was, and that, if she could but once attract her attention, the rest would follow. She had undoubtedly arranged the meeting with Miss Thompson, and so in train the course of events which resulted in our becoming convinced of Survival. We realized later how those on the Other Side can plan ahead to bring about desired results.

"After she had ceased speaking, my wife heard a whistle, which she recognized as that used by us when we became separated from our children in a crowd and wished to get together. Then our son spoke and gave many evidential details to prove his identity, also particulars of his passing, which had been unknown to her. He had been a young officer on the Field Artillery, and had been killed soon after the battle of Neuve Chapelle. (see note at end of section below-Ed) A long an intimate talk followed, which filled her with happiness such as she had never expected to experience again.

"After this a number of our friends and relatives came and spoke, and in all cases were able to convince her of their identity.

"At the end, a most remarkable thing occurred. There was a slight pause, and then both Brenton and Cecily etherealized in front of my wife from the waist up, my son in his full uniform, showing his medals, including the Military Cross, and on his shoulder the third star of a captain-a rank to which he had been gazette only two days before he was killed, and which he had never had the opportunity of wearing on earth. They stood there, nodding and smiling at her for fully two minutes.

"The etherialization,[21] which was seen by all three, must not be confused with materialization, although both are objective phenomena. The former is two-dimensional, just as are figures on the screen, whereas the latter is solid and substantial. Mrs. Wriedt, we had learned, had not had this form of phenomena for a number of years, but it appeared later that my wife had latently strong power for psychical phenomena. Mrs. Thompson also was a strong psychic, and the harmonious conditions which prevailed and the combined psychic powers of the three enabled our children to build up the ectoplasm given off and manifest in this manner.

"You can well imagine my wife's joy, and her great desire that I should enjoy a similar experience. She said to Mrs. Wriedt: "You simply must let my husband come and have a sitting." And the medium was so pleased at the return of her former power, she immediately consented, and a sitting was fixed for a few days later. When she returned home and told me of her experiences I looked at her quizzically, thinking that she had been hypnotized or was suffering from hallucinations. However, my interest was sufficiently aroused for me to agree to accompany her.

"Although I knew that my wife was extremely critical and of a well-balanced mind, it was difficult for me to believe that she had actually

---

[21] Etherialzation, a form of materialization but not as substantial and the form is semi-transparent and can usually be seen through.

seen and heard what she described, so I went to the sitting in a very skeptical spirit, with the full determination of keeping fully alert and on the lookout for anything of a suspicious nature. At this sitting, not only did our children come and talk with me, but also a number of my relations and officers whom we had known, giving proof of identity.

"One quite unexpected communication was from Brenton's special friend in his battery, whom I will call "K," and who had written to my wife after our boys passing. He himself had been killed in Mesopotamia six months later. He gave his name and spoke very clearly, and said that they were together once more. Much of the conversations with our children was of too personal a nature to quote, but the following are examples of a general nature:

"Brenton asked his mother if she had succeeded in finding his watch, which was missing from his kit which was returned to us in Malta, and referred to correspondence we had carried on with his bankers with the final setting up of his account. Cecily also referred to her long illness, saying that it was much better she had passed over, as, if she had lived, she would have been a constant sufferer. She said, "Mother, do not blame the doctor. He did quite right." This was very evidential, as my wife had a very hard feeling against the doctor, after being told by another surgeon that the operations she had undergone was not necessary. The medium had no possible means of knowing any of these circumstances.

"Finally, there as a short pause, as at the previous sitting, and Brenton etherealized in front of me, this time at full length, saying, "Do you see me dad?" and Cecily appeared in front of her mother. I came away from that sitting quite convinced of the actuality of Survival, and that our children had talked with us once more, a thing which we had never credited as being possible.

"Mrs. Wriedt, finding that we were such good sitters, since it turned out that I also was a strong battery of power and consequently caused no depletion of her psychic energy, made a special point of arranging further sittings for us whenever she had the time to spare. She would telephone to us, and we would go to her at very short notice, so as to avail ourselves as much as possible of her remarkable gift before her return to the U.S.A.

With each successive sitting our children became more proficient in communicating, their voices stronger and more like when on earth.

"I will not deal with each sitting seriatim, but have selected certain communications and incidents of an evidential nature, of general interest or having some special bearing upon the life or character of the communicator.

"After my first sitting, I decided to take down the details of each as fully as possible. As I did not know shorthand, I contrived to write in the dark in abbreviated longhand, transcribing it as early as possible whilst everything was fresh in our memories.

"Through the great kindness of Lord Methuen, Cecily had finally been brought to England in a hospital ship, landed at Plymouth, and taken to a nursing home, where she passed away a few days after my return from special duty in Egypt, whence I had been recalled by wire as her passing was imminent.

"We had subsequently arranged with a celebrated sculptor at Genoa to carve a beautiful memorial of Carrara marble to place over her grave. It had been erected just before our first sittings and we had not seen it. Besides having Cecily's epitaph upon it in bronze lettering, we had arranged that Brenton's name and particulars should also be placed upon it with the remark "Buried in Flanders."

"In speaking to Cecily about it, she told us where it had been made, commented upon its beauty, said that we should find that it had been properly erected where we went to see it, and added, "I am so happy that brother is sharing it with me." She told her mother that she was not to feel sad when she visited it, as she would be by her side. At that first sitting she spoke to me in Italian in response to remarks made by me in that language. She also spoke in French.

"One afternoon my wife left her room at the Theosophical Club, where we were then living, to meet me and go to a sitting. During a conversation with Brenton, he said, "Mother, I see you have a new blue bedspread on your bed." My wife replied, "No dear, I have no blue bedspread. What makes you think I have?" He answered, "Oh, I just blew in on my way here, and I saw it in your room." My wife then suddenly remembered that she had bought some blue silk that morning to re-line a kimono and she had spread it over her bed to see if it was sufficient. In her haste to go to the sitting she had left it like that, and to a boy it would appear to be a coverlet.

"Almost immediately after our first sittings, we began to see spirit lights and pulsating clouds of various colors. My wife became very clairsentient, and began to feel touches. At the sittings she arranged with the children that they should touch her on the face. She was thus able to arrange, by a simple code, one touch for "yes," and two for "no," for answers to be given to questions which could be replied to in that way. She used to lie down to rest after lunch and ask the children questions aloud. This had a curious sequel.

"At a sitting, Cecily said, "Mother, you must not speak to me aloud in your room as you do. Servants and guests going past your door and hearing you speak, apparently to yourself, will begin to think you are queer. There is no need to speak aloud, ask your questions mentally, and I shall get them."

"We has (*sic*) so many lovely talks with our dear ones that my wife especially seemed to be living in a seventh heaven, and spent much of her time in dwelling in thought upon her experiences and talking with them. This eventually brought a sharp reprimand from Dr. Sharp, who told her, "you must not be selfish, and think your children can always come, but others are with you to help. You must not always be dwelling in the spirit world. You must come down to the earth plane. You have to live your life on earth."

"My wife explained that she was anxious to speak with the children as often as possible, as we were shortly going to Scotland, Mrs. Wriedt was leaving and she feared that she would then have no further opportunities of doing so. Dr. Sharp replied, "You will find someone when you go to Scotland. An Egyptian guide is treating you for your nerves." He then gave me a prescription for an old fashioned herbal remedy, which we were to have made up on the way home, and which she was to take. This we did, and, as the chemist was preparing it, we wondered what he would think if we informed him that it had been prescribed by a spirit doctor.

"My mother had passed on in 1921, and, at her request, I had arranged for her cremation. She stated that this method was much preferable to ordinary burial. She said, "When one is buried, one's people are always coming to see the grave, and it makes us sad to see then grieving when we cannot comfort them. When one is cremated, this is to a large extent avoided."

"This was the first spiritualistic public service we ever attended, and after the address, Mr. Vout Peters[22] gave clairvoyance. We were absolutely unknown to anyone in the hall. "Throughout the service my wife, through her newly developed clairvoyance, was aware of Brenton's

---

[22] Alfred Vout Peters (1867-1934), British trance and clairvoyant medium. He figured prominently in Oliver Lodge's book *Raymond*. His mediumship began in 1895 when he attended a séance. His spirit control was "Moonstone" He was involved in the Spiritualist movement for more than 37 years.

presence. The medium selected us for his first message, and described Brenton in great detail, adding that he had been very athletic and very fond of horses. This was quite true. He stated that Brenton had come not so much with the desire of being described, as to give my wife the message, "There was no need to worry about the lady." My wife had been worrying about her mother's health, as she was quite old, and Brenton had informed her at one of the sittings that his grandmother was not very well. It was noticeable that he did not mention either her name or relationship, but he had always been reticent. Brenton also called attention to Cecily's birthday the following month, and said they wanted us to be cheerful and happy, as they would be with us.

"At the next sitting with Mrs. Wriedt, Brenton referred to the foregoing incident, and said that he was often with the horses. I asked him, "Is it really true that you have horses over there?" He replied, "Yes father. It is like this. We have all the animals that we love. Horses, dogs, cats and birds—only in etheric form."

"This was corroborated at another sitting by Cecily, who said that she had brought "Kouse-Kouse," her favorite Persian cat, which she had had in Malta. Shortly after we heard two sneezes and a bark through the trumpet. Cecily told us that it was our little foxterrier "Sandy," who had been killed in Malta. My wife said, "If that is Sandy, Bark!"—and a sharp bark was heard. Again: "Is that you Sandy? If so, give a louder and stronger bark." This was immediately done.

"One day Brenton's friend "K" came through whistling "I'll 'tak' the high road and you'll 'tak' the low road," and addressing me said, "I hear you are going to Scotland. "This was a great surprise to me, as I did not receive official notice of my appointment to Rosyth Dockyard until some days later. On several occasions we heard one spirit speaking through the trumpet, another in the "direct voice," and the medium speaking simultaneously. The final sitting with Mrs. Wriedt was on the eve of our departure for the U.S.A., when she came to our room at the Theosophical Club. If I had had any doubt before as to the genuineness of her powers, it would have been dispelled after this occasion.

"We had arranged the furniture, and we two, our friend Miss Thompson and the medium sat in the space between our two beds. We had provided our own trumpet for use in addition to her own, and we were close enough to have noticed at once any manipulation of the trumpets or simulation by her of the spirit voices.

"We had noticed before her arrival that there was much psychic power, and the room became filled with golden-hued pulsating clouds.

We fully anticipated an extra good sitting, and we were certainly not disappointed.

"The time was devoted to talks by our children and my mother, mainly on subjects of personal interest, and to our approaching removal to Scotland, whilst Miss Thompson had messages from her father and brother.

"Cecily was in a specially happy mood, so that we could almost feel joy radiating from her. She sang a song of her own composition in a very beautiful manner.

"There was one rather humorous incident. After my mother had finished speaking, my wife remarked, "I wonder of Brenton has gone." The answer came, "No, mother I am still here. I am on dad's bed just behind you. Mother thinks we are dashing in an out all the time."

"Brenton also confirmed that his face was on the first Armistice photo taken by Mrs. Deane, and a copy of which Miss Stead had given my wife. He indicated the position where he was to be found, as well as that of his friend "K" who had not been so successful as he in showing himself clearly.

"Thus came to an end the series of sittings which gave us an invaluable introduction into Spiritualism, and for which we shall ever owe a deep debt of gratitude to Mrs. Wriedt. It started with a friendship with her which has lasted to the present day.

"We felt sad that they had ended all too soon, and wondered whether we should find any medium in Scotland from whom we should obtain such comfort as we had received from this wonderful little American woman.

"At one of the early sittings Cecily told us that if we went to Mrs. Deane for a sitting on her birthday, she would try and give us a more beautiful psychic picture than that on Mrs. Thompson's photograph.

"We did so, and the exposure was made for ten minutes on a Paget colored plate-we watched all the processes to assure ourselves that there was no fraud. The result was one of the best and clearest psychic photographs ever taken, and shows Cecily absolutely full of vitality, in marked contrast to her condition for so long before passing. We sat a second time, and Brenton's face appeared, but he forgot to open his eyes, and his face looked so sad, as if he carried the thought of what he looked like at the time of his passing.

"We have presented many copies to Spiritualist organizations all over the world, and they have been greatly admired and proved excellent propaganda for the Cause."

The Battle of Neuve Chapelle (10–13 March 1915) took place in the First World War in the Artois region of France. The attack was intended to cause a rupture in the German lines, which would then be exploited with a rush to the Aubers Ridge and possibly Lille. A French assault at Vimy Ridge on the Artois plateau was also planned to threaten the road, rail and canal junctions at La Bassée from the south as the British attacked from the north. The British attackers broke through German defences in a salient at the village of Neuve-Chapelle but the success could not be exploited (Ed.).

Dr. JOHN S. KING:
DAWN OF THE AWAKENED MIND
DETROIT, 1911

"The truth was a mirror in the hands of God." ~ Rumi

Dr. John S. King

"This seance was held on Saturday night, 18th November, 1911, in Mrs. Wriedt's seance room, Detroit. The sitters were four women, a man, and a little boy, who together with myself made a circle of seven. I did not take copious notes as I usually did, but wrote my record after my return to the hotel. I do not therefore record all the facts, but briefly note interesting features which I deem worthy of record as evidential in character. Dr. Sharp, the control of Mrs. Wriedt, greeted me, and in doing so, reminded me that he had fulfilled the promise he had made me in this same seance room last Sunday, the 12th November, to visit the Jonson seance on the night I would have my surprise. He had promised that he would materialize in the cabinet, walk out, and place his hand on my head, and I would know by that act, that it was he (Dr. Sharp). I admitted to his medium, Mrs. Wriedt, and before all the sitters, that Dr. Sharp had fully and successfully carried out his promise, exhibiting much strength when he placed his hand on my head. That occasion was the second one where Dr. Sharp appeared materialized in my presence.

"In my records of August 7, 1910, I find this entry, which mentions him, viz. "At the private seance this Saturday forenoon, 7th August, 1910, Mrs. Jonson sat with Mrs. King (then in mortal life) and myself, we three being all in room B, while Jonson was lying on a couch in room A, the other side of the curtain, which filled the space left for a door. After several forms had materialized, a form claiming to be that of Dr. Sharp, a heavy set, and well bearded intelligent-looking old man, called on me, and said, while he stood in the materialized form, "As you are an old friend of my medium, Mrs. Etta Wriedt of Detroit, I felt I would like to call on you." We (my wife, then living, and myself) bade him welcome, and after a short conversation he withdrew.

"The same seance which Dr. Sharp attended in materialized form, above recorded, was rendered memorable to me for several reasons which merit recognition, and may hold connection with events of prior date, as well as with others of later date in this volume, which even now, or probably in the near future, will by association with other dates, events, facts, or statements, prove to be circumstantial evidence, or corroborative testimony, hence will be noted in the foregoing connection. "Otelleo," another intelligence, who has held communication with me for years, through various mediums, and as varied phases, having first materialized and conversed with me, through this same medium (J. B. Jonson) in another place in 1907, as he was about to retire promised to return, and bring with him a distinguished personality that I would be pleased to meet. He retired and shortly after returned with an alleged friend and brother, and introduced one alleged "Hiram Abiff." My guide, Hypatia, who has always alleged that she was the daughter of Theon, and consequently as such would be known as the Neoplatonic philosopher, visited us and then retired, but before doing so promised to return and did in a little while re-enter with another beautiful angelic young woman, whom she introduced to my wife as Saphrona.

"This same 7th of August, 1910, seance was made memorable, by the conditions imposed and accepted, at the time of our presentation to Hypatia of white roses, tied in my case with a bow of white satin baby ribbon, and in the case of my then wife, May, tied in a bow with blue satin baby ribbon, and which is more fully referred to in two other chapters covering the present series of seances, viz.: at Detroit through the trumpet, and on Wednesday night, the 15th November, 1911, at Jonson's, on both occasions by Hypatia, who retained the roses one year, three months and eight days before returning them to me, tied as when she received them, and looking as fresh, and my wife as spirit was present when she did so.

"The next intelligence to address me at Mrs. Wriedt's seance of 18th November, 1911, was Grey Feather, the alleged Indian control of J. B. Jonson, in Toledo, who gave me two reasons for coming to this seance, the first being, that he promised May Donna would come, and he now kept that promise, and the second being a matter of solely personal and private interest, which would serve no useful purpose to make record of here. May, my spirit wife, followed Grey Feather, and not only endorsed what Grey Feather said, but went more into details. Hypatia spoke about the same matter as did Grey Feather, and May, but spoke more earnestly and advisedly than was usual with her. The attitude and earnestness of these three spirit witnesses in their several communications to me, touching a matter of personal interest, supplied evidential matter of a most convincing kind, but unavailable here. Another feature of this seance was the singing by two different voices separately of Scotch melodies, and a few stanzas of well-known hymns. One of the sitters received very much advice from some alleged spirit speaking through the trumpet, regarding an intricate business matter, which became very interesting to her, though of no evidential value to me. My alleged spirit daughter's name (May Donna), as I received it at the Jonson seance, was announced, with the addition "Only to let you know that I am here, Papa."

"At this seance the very ancient guide—with a very long name, which I could not write down nor pronounce, nor remember after he had materialized at the fifth seance of the series at Jonson's, but who was by me to be designated, and known for the present, as Asia,—came. As he spoke without announcing his name, the question asked was, "Who is this?" After a brief pause there came in thundering tones the word or name "Asia." He had some years ago made himself known as an ancient spirit guide of mine. He spoke slowly in the English language, and informed me that he had now come to begin the work that he had on the first and only occasion, about six years previously, indicated through another medium, and that he would talk with me again when I sat alone.

"The alleged spirit of a little Indian girl who said her name was " Pansy," and that she came to see Big Chief, enlivened matters for fully fifteen minutes, creating much laughter, which became more or less contagious from her own. She also created some amusement at my expense, and set me guessing. She said she was in my home, Toronto, and "your squaw (meaning my wife's photograph) was on your office table."I was at first puzzled to know what she meant. She apparently enjoyed my stupidity for the moment, and laughed heartily and said, "Your squaw stands by you now."

"Then I realized that part, when it dawned on me that I had left my late wife's picture on my table with that of a friend. So I said, " Now tell me if she is anywhere else," and she told me where three of her pictures hung on walls and a photograph picture on the dresser. She described the location of each as I found them on my return home. They, with all the hangings, had been changed during my absence, and I had not absolutely definite fixture of these in my mind, and though I knew the position of some of them, before the change, I could not give their relative positions with adjacent pictures, after the change, which she had done I think under the circumstances, the hypothesis of thought transmission or mind reading in this case would be far-fetched.

"After my return home I was able to verify the absolutely correct location and situation of the pictures, as she had stated in the séance, and am able therefore to include in this connection my acknowledgement of the correctness of what was described in the hearing of all who participated in the seance. So that the testimony given in the seance was confirmed as correct from my comparison of the testimony with the existing facts.

"The seventh and last seance of the November, 1911, series was held during the forenoon of November 19th at the home of Mrs. Etta Wriedt, and was absolutely private, save and except for the presence of this very exceptional psychic.

"This seance proved to be, to me, one of the most important, if not absolutely the most relatively important, of all the seances I have ever attended in my life up to the present time, and at the same time most deeply interesting, and evidentially convincing, leaving not even a lingering doubt in my mind, as to May having kept her promise and redeemed her bond. Taking into consideration the many evidential matters presenting, from the intercommunion between various members of the family connections of mine, and myself, and the various attitudes of individual relatives one toward another, to all intents and purposes, the private family talk, with the attitude assumed by one and another, regarding this or that circumstance, all so realistic and true to the knowledge I possessed, even to minutiae, and the apparently harmonious condition, and happy relationship experienced by each and everyone, as well as the confirmations of previous evidential matter, facts and messages, together with the presentation of new evidential matter, and the clearing away of any fragments of ignorance, and my enlightenment as to many matters, while so satisfactory and convincing to me, cannot in the very nature of things be reproduced in this publication in detail, but only alluded to in the briefest outline.

"One reason for not reproducing family affairs in this publication is the fact that to most people, as well as to myself, it would appear as needless exposure of confidential knowledge, and another reason, as has been mentioned elsewhere, that May, my spirit wife, whose human personality she has established to my entire satisfaction, and as I have already said redeemed her bond,— expressed her desire that I should not use family matters when I had enough other material for my book. This request I shall show my respect for, by a faithful compliance therewith in matters of detail, or where it would prove inadvisable to repeat a message from one to another, or to use language which might be construed as personal. My alleged spirit daughter, who not only materialized as a young woman of about twenty years, but also spoke with me on the special occasion at Toledo, when I learned for the first time her name, as known in spirit life, and which occasion is elsewhere recorded as being the 15th November, 1911, seance at Jonson's, and who promised then, and at the last of the Jonson seances, to come with her mamma and myself to Detroit, and without a doubt she has fulfilled that promise, and was one of the first of the numerous intelligences, to speak to me through the trumpet at Mrs. Wriedt's. She gave me messages to be delivered to her brother and her sister (half-brother and half-sister), also told me that their mother Martha was present at the seance with her mamma, May.

"The next to converse with me was Martha E. King, my first wife, who passed to spirit realms about 37 years ago now, and who, on this occasion, talked with me, about our children, and also other matters. Then May joined in the conversation with Martha and me, and both of them were agreed and harmonious, and with one accord and single purpose, advised me as to my future course. Hypatia, my ever-present guide, joined in now, before the loved ones withdrew, and her first words were, "You wrote it correctly, tia' is right." To make clear the relation of this interjected sentence, I may say that the stenographer who made the report of the second seance at Jonson's for me, had in the report spelled my guide's name "Hypacia," which I corrected with my pen by changing the fifth letter to "t," thus making the word "Hypatia." A few minutes before going upstairs to the seance room, and while waiting to be called, I wrote the following on a page of my memo-book, and kept it exposed to her view until I started upstairs, when I put it in my pocket. "Hypatia, the stenographer spelt your name with last syllable 'cia' while I write it 'tia.' Which is correct?" The first exclamation was Hypatia's answer to my question, and was the first expression which she vocally gave in my hearing. This was followed by advice, and instruction in regard to certain business matters. A short discussion of a particular situation was had by Hypatia, May and Dr. Sharp, the psychic's own control, and conclusion reached, that all would come out right by my maintaining the attitude I had assumed.

"The balance of the seance turned out to be a gathering of spirit guides, and many of them gave their instructions to me. There was also some prediction, and caution meted out to me, as well as information for me, and instruction what to do. My life was to be a new one, and still active I would be, for special work, in spirit spheres, was planning for me. From records which I now possess, I must select and gather more, and print a book. Then other books to follow this there'll be; and other work for me to do, of which I must be close, and much would be done for me. I cannot more than outline give, as I have done above. This chapter now will conclude a series; but still more evidence I will collect, and more truth I will proclaim."

CORROBORATIVE TESTIMONY
TORONTO CANADA
PUBLISHED BY JOHN S. KING

"Reports by Herbert G. Paull, Secretary, and by Rev'd Canon William Walsh, member of the Canadian Society for Psychical Research. A deceased member, 'Mrs. May E. King, wife of the President, visits a trumpet circle, in Toronto, held by Mrs. Etta Wriedt, trumpet medium, and speaks to those two members.'"

Dr. John S. King, President C. S. P. R.

Dear Sir:
"I herewith hand you a partial report of a trumpet seance held at the house of Mr. and Mrs. W., Toronto, on the evening of Monday, November 27, 1911. The seance was held in an attic room, with twenty-five sitters, and the medium, Mrs. Etta Wriedt. Among those present were the following members of the Canadian Society for Psychical Research, namely: Dr. John S. King, President, Rev'd Canon Wm. Walsh, Professor E. B. Shuttleworth, Mrs. Coleman, and the Secretary, Herbert G. Paull (the writer of this report).

"The circle was opened with a repetition of the Lord's Prayer in unison, followed by singing "Nearer My God to Thee," augmented by a powerful spirit voice through the trumpet. After a cordial introduction by the guide, Dr. Sharp, who evidently was able to give the names and idiosyncrasies of every sitter present, occasional whispering voices were heard and recognized by friends present. Presently a strong and clear voice spoke out near Canon Walsh.

Voice: "Canon Walsh. Canon Walsh:"

Yes, who is it?

Voice: "It is May. Canon Walsh"

What is your name?

Voice: "May E. King. I want to thank you for the kind and beautiful words you spoke over my body as it lay in the casket."

"The voice purporting to be that of Mrs. King, then continued in a lengthy, and touching strain, voicing her thanks and appreciation of Rev. Canon William Walsh's tribute to her memory, she having been a member of the Research Society, of which Rev. Canon Walsh is also a member. Again the same voice changed location to where I was sitting, and addressed me.

May E. King: "And you, Mr. Paull, I'm so pleased to see you here."

Mr. Paull: I am delighted to hear you indeed.

May E. King: "I am pleased to be here tonight. All is beautiful and bright over here. There is no death."

The writer cannot recall the exact words of what followed, but Mrs. King continued to speak cheerily of the spirit life, and spoke once at least of Dr. King as "Johnnie." Several other individual voices continued to speak through the trumpet, and then a whispering voice said, while the trumpet was directed to Dr. King.

Voice: "Papa."

Dr. King: Who is it for?

Voice: "For you, papa."

Dr. King: Is it you, my darling?

Mr. Paull: Tell us your name.

Voice: "May Donna."

May Donna: "Papa, Hypatia is here."

Dr. King: Will she sing for us tonight?

Mr. Paull: I do not recollect the exact reply.

May Donna: "Good-bye, papa."

Dr. King: Good-bye, darling, speak to us again.

The writer cannot set down with exactness what further was spoken, but subscribes to the above as a faithful account as he recalls it after the seance, and the conversations and communications between the voices purporting (and evidently being) the voices of Mrs. May E. King and her daughter, May Donna, both in spirit life."

(Signed) *Herbert G. Paull,*
Secretary C. S. P.

Dr. John S. King, President C. S. P. R.

Dear Sir:
"I send you my report of Mrs. Etta Wriedt's seance, held on the 27th of November, 1911, as follows" (corroborative testimony): [The Author's Note:—Following is another individual member's report of the same section of the trumpet seance as reported by the Secretary, Mr. Herbert G. Paull, and although the report as a whole was given much more extendedly, the quotation therefrom has a slightly different construction, though it is valuable in that there is harmony of facts in the reports of both, though neither is a stenographer. The Canon in his report says: "I had a small writing pad and by feeling was guiding myself in writing, as it was absolutely black darkness in the room, and straining my eyes and ears almost unconsciously I was stooping forward, trying to catch some faint sight or revealing sound, when this to me new, unexpected, and surprising episode took place. Now I was quietly startled by just a perceptible touch of the trumpet on my left eyebrow. At the instant there was suggested to my mind that it was done caressingly. From the trumpet, seemingly, in the center of the circle, and pointing towards me, came a strong whisper repeating my name. Then I said:
"Who is it?"
Voice: "May."
Then a voice, full, cultured, and clear, and which at once recalled to me the voice of Mrs. King, said: "Canon, I want to thank you for your kindness in coming and offering up a prayer before the casket was closed that day."
Then the trumpet seemed to move over in the direction of Dr. King and Mr. Paull, who were seated comparatively near together, and addressed them in similar tones, as they by their responses seemed to recognize. The words addressed to them I cannot recall, as I was so interested, excited, and thrilled by the recognition of Mrs. Dr. King's familiar and kindly voice, that I could not concentrate my attention upon them and their respective conversations with her.

"To me it was all the more startlingly striking in view of the fact that not long before I left the residence of Dr. John S. King (the President of our Society) accompanied by him, he wrote in his office on a slip of paper and showed it to me, as a request of his addressed to Mrs. King, using her Christian name, and when the trumpet voice spoke to me it was a direct response to, and compliance with, the written request at that moment remaining spread out on the table in the room we had just left to come to the seance, and some of the words and phrases of the trumpet voice were identical with those contained in the request. Surely the line of least resistance is to follow the exercise of our reasoning powers, and accept of the claimed fact, that the spirit of Mrs. Dr. King spoke through the trumpet consciously and intelligently, touching that very important episode—the removal from time to the spirit world, and the bearing away of the sacred body to be laid in the last resting-place."

(Signed) *William Walsh*

John S. King

First Trumpet Seance of December, 1912, Series, Detroit

"I reached Detroit on Friday afternoon, December 20, 1912. I phoned Mrs. Wriedt, and secured a sitting for 8 o'clock p.m. Her house was the one I visited before, but I had to reach it by a new car route. While on the car a coincidence presented. While standing in the aisle, because the seats were occupied. I asked a passenger who sat near to me, and whose eye I caught, Can you tell me where this car meets Baldwin Avenue?" He replied by first asking me, "What number do you want to find on Baldwin Avenue?" and when I told him, he then said, "That's where I am going now myself, and I will show you if you leave the car when I do." He did so, and found that he and another man along with us were booked for the seance. The one who entered the house with me had had about one year's experience at intervals of séances, while the third man whom we met there, and who helped to form our semi-circle in the seance room, had only sat once or twice before; and who, though fleshy, large and strong, was nervous, which he preferred to call anxiety. In this seance I received but a few demonstrations strictly intended for me, but had a few friendly talks with loved ones, and a guide or two; and my interests were otherwise divided between the efforts of inexperienced spirits, and the "anxiety "of the inexperienced man."

Second Trumpet Seance of December, 1912, Series

"This seance, by appointment, was held for me alone, on Saturday morning, December 21st. It was a lengthy sitting, and to me satisfactory, as my lone sittings usually are. As soon as the electric light was turned off in the room, the spirit lights appeared to view, and the demonstrations in the room were beautiful. Lights in all parts of the room appeared to view, and then a spirit brought the trumpet to me, and asked me to examine it, and as I looked into it, at the expanded end, I could see all through to where the mouthpiece was, and the whole of it illuminated, while I held it so that I could see the whole inside from end to end, aglow with light. Hypatia, my spirit guide, was the first to come, and she told me that my band of guides, and several of my loved ones were present with me, and that while May and some of my loved ones would talk with me, the guides would either talk with or sing for me.

"Hypatia was the first one to sing, and she gave a stanza or two of song, so loudly that she could be heard out in the street, Mrs. Wriedt, the medium, meanwhile remarking, "Oh, isn't that wonderful. Then the ancient guide Asia, as I have named him, came. He was on earth, as he alleges, nearly twenty thousand years before the Christian Era, at which time he claims North America was under water. Electra, sister of my guardian Egyptia, and an alleged member of my band came and spoke and sang. She sang loudly and distinctly, as did Cleopatra also. All three of these alleged themselves to be members of my spirit band. Then there also came Otelleo, and so there were in all six out of seven of the alleged members of my spirit band, each one of whom spoke as loud as I do when I am speaking to other persons. All these alleged guides have materialized for me at the Jonson's on several occasions, and two or three with other mediums, and conversed with me while presenting to me in their transient bodies. Each one of them has also written messages to me, through the Human-Psychic Telephone.[23] Both

---

[23] The Human Psychic Telephone: Mrs. Maud Venice Gates, a native of New York State; Professionally, a teacher, genealogist and nurse. An outstanding Automatic Writing/Speaking medium who discovered her gift in 1892 through the use of a Quija board.

Egyptia and Electra appeared to me materialized at the seances held by Effie Moss at London, more than twenty years ago; and some fourteen years thereafter, they again appeared in form, when Mrs. Moss was holding seances at Lily Dale.

"Both of these spirits also came together and walked around the circle of relatives and friends, to whom I introduced them. This was at a seance held by Nichols at Lily Dale, some years ago (in 1908), when some members of the Canadian Society for Psychical Research, and a few other selected friends, held a seance under test conditions, one of which was that the medium lay on his back, upon the floor within the cabinet, while the heavy vice-president stood astride of him, as the various forms materialized, including Egyptia, and Electra, who claim to have been my guardian spirits from the time I was born, and were familiar to the view of May, my spirit wife, while still in her mortal life, and since then they now attend upon her necessities, as she herself tells me in her messages through the writing psychic to me, though on the first occasion that Electra was materialized, she was brought into the seance at Jonson's by Hypatia in the presence of the selected company.

"Gray Feather, the strong Indian control of J. B. Jonson, the materializing medium of Toledo, came and spoke with me at this trumpet seance to tell me, that Jonson was coming home, and he wanted me to come down there on Monday afternoon. This same Indian control Gray Feather, in my presence in a former Jonson seance in April last, announced the arrival of Stead in spirit land, and told the listeners who were present there with me, 'that he had visited and talked with Stead in life in Julia's Bureau, in England. Gray Feather also on his own initiative wrote through the hand of a writing psychic, and urged me to meet him on a certain day and at a certain place, in New York State, of which a record appears elsewhere, and when I did so he brought the late Judge Rose of Toronto to speak to me, which was the first and only time that Judge Rose had thus spoken with me, though he wrote a message on a slate for me, and signed it. I have it also recorded in a previous chapter that he, Gray Feather, controlled, on two separate days, another trumpet medium instead of her own acknowledged control. He not only spoke through that trumpet himself, but brought on those occasions thirty-one spirit personalities to speak with me. May has acknowledged, when sending messages to me, that this noble Indian spirit has often been a strong helper to her."

Third Trumpet Séance of December, 1912, Series

"I remained in my room at the hotel till nearly noon, the 22nd day of December, then I went by invitation to a friend's home for dinner, and finally reached Mrs. Wriedt's at 3.30 p. m., the time appointed for my seance. I had my sitting not alone, but with one gentleman whom I never met before. MacRoberts, at whose home in London the Moss seances were held over twenty years ago, came at this seance and talked on several subjects with me. The communication was interesting and among other things he said to me, "Doctor, you have outlived most of the boys." It will be noted that this and other two of the four seances were what is known as mixed circles, where both time and interest are divided between the sitters, and the share is lessened which comes to each one, though opportunities are all the time presenting for investigating and considering conditions, and estimating the relationship of conditions presenting and results obtained, as well as observing the effect of harmonious conditions. One unexpected caller from the spirit land was a man well known in my city, and likewise a man of wealth, who lost money, caste and influence, on account of acquired habits undesirable in character; and his language and tone of speech were sad when he spoke with me, as he was aware that I knew his habits.

"Among others who came and spoke with me, on matters of personal interest, or benefit, but not specially of public interest, was des Asia, my alleged ancient guide of the very long ago, who came and talked in English language, and told me much that I was pleased to know. And so it was with others of my guides, especially my chief spirit guide Hypatia, and also another one, Cleopatra. May Donna, my daughter, who passed to spirit life at birth more than twenty years ago, also made her presence known and now told me that when I reached Toledo she would again materialize and talk to me there.

"May came to me as usual, for she always does whenever I am with a psychic, and proves herself by calling me according to our ante-mortem agreement, by the test name "Johnnie." I had a good talk with May about her personal possessions, and what she suggested I had better do with everything, and she gave me her directions explicitly. May talked with me this time, I believe, without a trumpet, and said she had no suffering now, and I must try and be cheerful and enjoy myself, and that she was told I was to have splendid health and strength and live to be very old, and had most important work before me to accomplish. She also wished me Merry Christmas and a Happy New Year. Before she bid me good-bye she told me that she was going home tonight to see her mother, but would be here again with me at the morning seance at 8 o'clock. I may here add that when the spirits assume the transient bodies formed for them, they look as natural as in life, though the garments which are upon them may or may not resemble those worn by human ones; and they claim they are creations of their own desires."

Go forth to the world as an expositor of truth.

The Fourth Trumpet Séance, 1912 Series

"In the early morning of the 23rd of December, 1912, I had my sitting with another gentleman in the last trumpet seance of the season, which will be the last one also to be recorded in the book, which will go forth to the world as an expositor of truth, and upholder of the spiritual philosophy. The reader will remember that as reported in the seance preceding this one, that May said to me through the trumpet, that she was going to her mother's, after the seance, but would be back in time to meet me in the seance this morning. I entered the seance room feeling slightly chilly, and Mrs. Wriedt brought me a cup of hot coffee, remarking, "You are the man who drank the first cup of coffee in my seance room."

"When the coffee cup was empty, and the light turned off, a man's voice loud and natural said, "Good morning," and I enquired, "Who is this?" when May answered me, "Why, it is Pa." I then remarked, "Your coming is a great surprise, for this is the first time I have heard from you since you left your body many years ago," after which he gave through the trumpet his full name, as if to corroborate what May had said, and seemed to be overjoyed, at this his new-found mode of conversing. May was also very pleased on account of my surprise, as I did not know why she was going home, and something prevented my asking her. She probably knew that his inclinations would most likely take him there. All of this seemed very natural, and I had a good talk with both of them (father and daughter).

"May, while she was talking with me there, cried a most life-like cry, and said, "Oh, it makes me feel so sad, to see you all alone, and no one about you to do or care for you, when you were always so good and kind to me, and did everything you could for my benefit. I am near to you nearly all the while, though I cannot seem to impress you, by myself alone." Asia and Hypatia, two of my guides, came again, and Dr.

Sharp, control of Mrs. Wriedt, told me that Gray Feather, J. B. Jonson's strong Indian control, was busy gathering spirit bands, and forces, so that I might have the very best results along the lines I had in mind, especially so because Jonson was not strong in vitality. May Donna, my daughter, humorously remarked to me, "Sometime while you are at Jonson's, I'll walk out from the cabinet and kiss you." Cleopatra, as she alleges herself to be, and also claims to be a guide and aider, told me during the seance, that she would try and find an opportunity to materialize while at Jonson's.

"Stainton Moses, as he claimed to be, and whose name and fame are known to Englishmen, also made a call at this morning seance, and spoke quite unreservedly to me. I told him I would be glad to hear again from him, and communicate any message which he might have for his fellow-countrymen. Mrs. Effie Moss, the physical medium, I first met in London, Canada, at the MacRoberts home, was pleased once more to come from spirit sphere and talk with me, and thanked me for all I said and did for her, and for her manager, at the time they had their trouble there some twenty years ago. MacRoberts' alleged guide, Cynthia, also came and talked with me. Dr. Sharp, Mrs. Wriedt's control, then spoke a word or two, before he closed the seance, and in doing so, said, before you leave Toledo I will be down to show myself, as I always admire, and like to honor you.

"One feature of this seance, as well as of some others, has developed a circumstance of importance, inasmuch as it has helped to unfold a secret which has been withheld for many years, and establishes, beyond any doubt, all the three contentions claimed by me, viz.: 1st, Continuity of Life, 2nd, Spirit Return, and 3rd, Spirit Communion, and to this may now be added Prophesy. The personalities concerned will in no way be disclosed, but the circumstances I will now relate in support of my repeated contention made in tripartite as above. Many years ago, there resided in my city a man, his wife and family, together with a sister of the wife. His means were ample, and occupation and reputation were both good. The wife and family were sent to the summer residence, while the husband and father remained, as did the sister of his wife.

"The time was fast approaching when an event of importance and of anxiety was due to most certainly transpire. It came and so did I as doctor, and I was therefore present at the birth of a son to the father, this well-known citizen, and the mother, who was a sister of his wife. In brief, the boy was illegitimate, and had come to stay, and whatsoe'er was said or done, it must be kept a secret by the doctor and the two concerned. A foster-mother was soon found, and the boy was well cared for. Everything ran quite smoothly, and the secret was not divulged.

"A few years elapsed, and then the father of this growing lad took ill, and passed out of the body to spirit realm. On two or three occasions prior to the present seance, the spirit of that father came and conversed with me through a trumpet, about his anxiety of mind regarding the past and the future of this illegitimate son. He told me that he had made provision for the boy's education and advancement, and had placed it with the mother of the boy to be administered, but she did not evince an interest of earthly mother character, but preferred that he would go to heaven. He has not, however, gone to that place, in accordance with her wish, as will be realized by further reading. At the present seance, the spirit of the father again came and spoke with me, and told me exactly where I could find his boy, and how and where he was employed, and that he had grown to be a man. He asked me to divulge the secret to the boy of his true parentage, and let him know of what was placed with the mother for his benefit, before he, the father, had gone out of the physical. He also said that he would try and bring the boy and me together, and let me know the address of the mother.

"The latter part of this strange foregoing communication was made to me in the seance room at Mrs. Wriedt's in Detroit on the morning of 23rd December, 1912."

MRS. PHILLIP CHAMPION DE' CRESPIGNY: THIS WORLD AND BEYOND WIMBLEDON, LONDON ENGLAND, 1914

Mrs. Phillip Champion De'Crespigny

"Then, not long before the machines of war ripped their way through the peace of nations, and turned life into temporary chaos, I met Mrs. Etta Wriedt. It was in May 1914!

"Everyone with any knowledge of this subject of psychic research knows Mrs. Wriedt as a celebrated medium for the direct voice. Her home is in Detroit, but at one time she spent a great deal of time in London and was well-known to all the prominent pioneers of the moment at that time. To her I owe one of the greatest privileges of my life—my first introduction to Sir Oliver Lodge, who has many a time extended a helping hand when I have been floundering in doubt or difficulty.

"I was introduced to Mrs. Wriedt by a man who at the time was a mere acquaintance, afterwards developing into an intimate friend— the late Colonel E. R. Johnson, who knew nothing of my life in the past, had never met my husband and who first mentioned Mrs. Wriedt's name to me in casual conversation. I may as well confess at once that I was full of prejudice, no objections on principle, nor disbelief in the possibility of communication, but I was 'up against' mediums in any form, connecting them with fraud, hoaxes and audiences of credulous people ready to swallow anything that came along, which latter is an attitude often adopted by persons toward others who happen to believe something they themselves do not!

"All I can say in extenuation is that I took the means at hand to correct these erroneous conclusions, and quickly realized that I was faced with a marvelous truth that every sense I possessed of logic, understanding and reason told me was fundamental and had been correct.

"I had disliked the very word medium although now I know no other term so aptly describes the living organism that appears to be the link between physical, etheric and astral conditions—the intermediary wavelength that can contact both worlds. Every known force in nature requires a medium through which it can make itself manifest; without it our senses are unaware of its existence. Electricity, magnetism, gravitation must have a means of manifestation. Seances, sittings, circles were all terms which in my ignorance were the expression of the entire gamut of trickery and imposition, but in spite of that I was ever conscious of the inborn conviction that somewhere lay the clue to communication between ourselves and those who had passed on to another world—a common-sense world of some kind, unconnected with harps and wings, and that if we could only put our hand on the key we could open the door. It was something impossible to put into words—an echo perhaps that clung to me and had come with me into this life from somewhere else?

"So, as I was always ready for adventure, I felt the experiment could do no harm even if it led to nowhere, through the kind offices of Colonel Johnson a sitting was arranged, my name being kept in the background, and on a fine bright day in May I found myself at a house in Wimbledon which I learnt later had once belonged to Mr. W. T. Stead. The knowledge of technical procedure in psychical research has so advanced during the last twenty years, and experiences in the seance-room become so widespread that it seems superfluous to go into a detailed description of the conditions under which my first seance was held, but as I hope to interest readers who perhaps have not been able to gain first-hand experience for themselves, I will give a brief description of the technical differences between a "direct voice" seance and that of the variety known as "trance."

"Etta Wriedt never went into trance, so far as I know. She remained throughout the sitting her fully conscious self, entering into the conversations in her ordinary voice, remembering afterwards all that had taken place, and on many occasions overlapping with her own conversation the voices of communicators trying to "come through."

"On this first occasion we were alone, in a large room empty of furniture beyond the chairs we sat on—I think there was a sofa in one corner of the room—with a distance of five or six feet between us, and the aluminum trumpet—used to assist those operating on the other side in concentrating the vibrations, as a megaphone is used here—at my feet between myself and Mrs. Wriedt.

"The room was darkened, an essential with this medium in obtaining the best result, for the same reason that a wireless message will travel considerably farther at night than in the daytime. The action of light has a destructive effect on ectoplasm and all phenomena dependent upon the use of it, and as the movements of the trumpet and no doubt the "larynx" formed by the unseen operators and instrumental in the transmission of the voices involve the use of this tenuous substance thrown out by the physical body, darkness is of the greatest assistance in this form of demonstration.

"At the same time the phenomenon has been produced in my own room when conditions made it impossible to exclude the light completely, and I have seen the levitation and movement of the trumpet take place without human contact of any kind. Mrs. Murphy Lydy,[24] a direct voice medium also well-known in America, produced the voice successfully in full daylight. It was rather a weird experience, sitting in the pitch dark with a total stranger waiting for—I hardly knew what!

---

[24] Murphy-Lydy, Mary (ca. 1870–?)
American materialization and trumpet medium, who practiced for many years in Chesterfield Camp, Indiana. She was engaged for a year by the Indiana Psychic Research Society at Indianapolis, toured the United States, and attained prominence in 1931 in England by platform demonstration of direct voice. Her chief controls were "Dr. Green" and "Sunflower."

"But once the communications began the commonplaceness of the situation and the voices robbed the phenomenon of any feeling of ghostliness or uncanniness. I did not recognize the voices, but the explanation of that is simple enough. The difference in tone of physical voices is due to the formation of the organs through which they are produced, and as these organs disintegrate with the physical body, the physical voice as we knew it can never be counted on in the different conditions. Some people, I believe, do recognize some of the voices that come through, but I say frankly I have never done so. Mannerisms, tricks in expression and so on continue and can be identified, I once recognized an uncle by his laugh before he gave me his name.

"Very shortly after the light was turned out I was touched on the knee, Mrs. Wriedt still talking from the same spot five or six feet away, and immediately afterwards I heard a voice speaking through the trumpet. It was a physical voice and would have been audible to any number of persons had they been in the room. There was no question of imagination or telepathy; it was an objective voice, and as Mrs. Wriedt continued to talk, I was obliged to ask her to desist as someone was trying to speak.

"Mrs. Wriedt described a figure she saw come into the room, a good description of my husband "in dark blue uniform with gold lace and shiny things on the shoulders." (Epaulettes.) She said he was dancing— we had both been very fond of dancing—and before he spoke a bar from our favorite waltz "Daheim" was whistled through the trumpet!

A Marvel Greater Than the Birth of The Steam Engines

"A voice then that claimed to be that of my husband spoke. He called me by my Christian name and seemed to be greatly agitated, but as it was not like my husband's voice, and moreover spoke with a pronounced American accent, it was not surprising that I doubted the identity of the speaker! Elucidation has to come gradually. But although in the first flush of a novel experience, and ignorance of the laws governing the situation, I doubted the claims of the speaker, I knew myself to be face to face with a marvel greater than the birth of steam engines, airplanes or anything yet discovered by the ingenuity and perseverance of mankind.

"I was up against" the most marvelous incident in my life! The voice spoke for some time asking and answering questions, the answers seemed to me a little illusive, unsatisfying. I wanted proof indubitable—complete. We all do—incontrovertible proof, that will save us the trouble of further doubt and inquiry—proof, that we shall never get without patience and persistent seeking.

"I wanted to set my own tests, a line of action and a frame of mind that always seems to inhibit the best results. Patience and a certain attitude of tolerance when things do not go exactly as we expect, hardly ever fail to bring proof in the end. That, at least, is my experience, but the evidence must be furnished by the operators on the other side in their own way. To attempt to impose our way on them while we are so ignorant of their limitations generally ends in disaster.

"After this, another voice claimed recognition, giving a Christian and surname which at first were unintelligible. Finally the speaker explained who he was by reference to my husband by a name that only a few members of his family had used, and I recognized him as a brother-in-law who had passed over as the result of an accident at polo fifteen years previously.

"I was much surprised. I considered him one of the most unlikely people to speak to me, but I asked what he was doing and if he was happy.

"Quite happy," he replied. "I am studying the subject of evolution and am much interested in all such subjects now."

"I have always been interested in natural science," I replied.

"Yes, I know, but I never expected to find you here."

"Why not?" I asked.

"Communication with another world has always seemed to me one of the solvable problems of the future."

"Well, you are the only member of the family who has tried to speak to us."

"That was true, but might have been a guess. He then went on to remind me of a dance we had been to when we were both young and of some flowers I had worn. Which was correct. He added, my husband had asked him to come through and assure me it was he who had spoken first.

"I had other visitors, including one who, although a stranger to me on this plane, has since become a valued link with the other. She said she was Florence Nightingale and showed me her lamp as an "identification mark"—the Lady of the Lamp. It was a luminous disk about the size of a bicycle lamp and as sharply defined. She waved it several times close to my face and I put out my hand and passed it right through the light. A case of fools stepping in where angels fear to tread! I certainly would not do such a thing now. I left Mrs. Wriedt's not satisfied. There is no need to deal with the usual objections urged by the novice, and which any ordinarily intelligent investigator is of course keeping in mind, such as—Ventriloquism?

"On one or two occasions Mrs. Wriedt was speaking at the same time as the voice through the trumpet. I had to ask her to stop. Also, I am told ventriloquism is not possible in the dark. Telepathy? At this first sitting this might have accounted for the matter of the communications, but not for the manner of conveying them. No one of any intelligence who has ever heard the direct voice in favorable circumstances will try to account for it through telepathy. It has no bearing on the problem. The subconscious mind?

"Even this overworked beast of burden may plead not guilty. The subconscious mind cannot—it is to be presumed—create an objective voice and, with telepathy, may be dismissed as of no assistance. The identity of the sitters remained the knotty point. Mrs. Wriedt might have been suspected of looking up family names, if by any chance she had managed to learn my own, and refer to members of my family correctly. There had been nothing absolutely convincing in anything that had taken place.

"In fact there had been a big error in a statement made. The voice alleged to be that of my husband had said, among other things, "Thank you for the flowers!" I, wishing to make my own tests, replied:

"Do you mean flowers I put on your grave?" and I thought the answer had been "Yes" which was quite wrong! Yet, there were points that required a good deal of explaining away. I went over the evidence carefully bit by bit, weighing the pros and cons with as little prejudice as possible, convinced only upon one point. Whoever their owners might be, the circumstances of my surroundings and my own common sense indicated that the voices came from that country from which Shakespeare in direct contradiction of the Bible, has told us there is no return.

"There seemed to be no other explanation—if my ordinary senses were of any use to me at all! And in the main they had spoken of affairs that could not possibly have been known to the medium. My first argument took a more or less negative form. If any person could communicate from the other side, my husband should be equally able to do so, and if he could, he would—a point those who have lost anyone for whom they greatly care would do well to consider.

"But—and it was a big but in those first days of uncertainty—the voice was not his voice, and he had made little mistakes in diction and phrases it was difficult to account for. I had not learnt then, as I have already explained, that the timbre, the actual ring of the old voice had presumably gone forever. But my brother-in-law, who had given his name and referred to trivial incidents that could not have been known to the medium, nor found in any reference book—how was he to be explained?—and how about the bar of "Daheim" that had been whistled as an introduction? Thought-reading? But that was merely suggesting a fresh miracle to account for the first, and anyway it did not explain the voices—nor the whistling. With so much uncertainty in my mind it might have been a long time before I visited Mrs. Wriedt again. I should have done so eventually, because I was puzzled—and when you have an inquiring mind you are not content to remain so, but the following day Colonel Johnson, whom I have already mentioned, spoke to me after a Theosophical meeting.

"He had visited Mrs. Wriedt that morning, had taken notes of the message on the spot, being an expert at doing so in the dark, and written them out afterwards. 'T' I don't know what it means," he explained, "but was told you would understand, and I give it to you verbatim." A voice, it seemed, had spoken to him from the trumpet in a state of great agitation, giving my husband's Christian and surnames, saying his wife had been there the previous day and had gone away doubting his identity, that she had misunderstood him, and he was most anxious Colonel Johnson should put it right. He said her father, Sir Cooper Key, was there, very happy and they had spent many hours together.

"He then said most earnestly: "She misunderstood me—she thought I said she put flowers on my grave. But it was her mistake. I have no grave. My body was cremated."

He then added: "It is very difficult to do this—as difficult as she found her painting when she first began. Ask her," he went on, if she remembers the Galaton—on the Australian Station. This will be understood."

"I am sorry I mismanaged it. (The seance.) We often do the first time."

"It is quite impossible to describe the overwhelming flood of conviction this message brought! It was as a crowning point of evidence after a lifetime of inquiry and honest speculation. I had been knocking all my life, and the door had at last opened. No one but my husband would have sent me that message. Those who have read the previous pages may understand the full force of it. The name of course should have been Galatea[25] showing how little Colonel Johnson understood the point of it.

[25] Galatea, in Greek mythology, a Nereid who was loved by the Cyclops Polyphemus. Galatea, however, loved the youth Acis. When Polyphemus discovered Acis and Galatea together, he crushed Acis to death with a boulder.

"None of it was known to the medium, nor to Colonel Johnson. Even if she had had the means of finding out so many details in my husband's life, she would only have had two days in which to do it. He had left the Navy thirty-four years previously, and to have suspected her of consulting ancient Navy lists, which are not at all easy to get at, would have been childish. Nor, if she had had the opportunity of doing so, would she have had any reason for selecting the Galatea among all the ships he had served in as of special interest. In its very triviality lay the weight of the evidence.

"At the séance, my husband had been followed, so Colonel Johnson said, by his own wife who had died some years before I made his acquaintance, and we had been unknown to one another during her earth life. She, too, sent me a message, to the effect that "Mrs. de Crespigny's father was present with her, and wished to say something about Malta, where she had been when she was a little girl." These messages, may it be noted, were brought to me by a third person, who knew nothing of my past life nor of the names given to him and passed on to me. They were not drawn from his subconscious mind as the information had never been known to him, and it was all sufficiently arresting to send me again to Mrs. Wriedt—this time to have all doubt removed, and to be convinced of a truth that is indeed the Pearl of great price.

"At the next sitting with Mrs. Wriedt my husband was preceded by his brother, who said the message about the Galatea had been sent to me as a proof of his identity, as he knew all it would convey to me, and he had been so distressed at having been previously misunderstood. My husband followed, called me by the old names and again mentioned the Galatea and did I remember how often he had told me of the good times they had?

Trivial? Of course, most of life is made up of trivialities. If he had told me the names of our children, the date of my marriage, or of his own death, the medium might have looked it up in a book, if he had given me a dissertation on philosophy, it would have been so unlike him I should not have believed in him at all, if he had described his life in that other world, I had first to be sure there was another world to describe. It was the reference to the little insignificant things in life—things known perhaps to him and me alone, that drove the truth home as could nothing else in the world. How would you prove your identity to someone who doubted it on the telephone?

"I remember a case in point. At the time the search for the poor little Lindbergh baby was going on, the Captain of the liner which had a short time before conveyed Colonel Lindbergh from England wished to speak to him on the telephone. Colonel Lindbergh, distracted, poor man, as he was, insisted upon the establishment of the communicator's identity before he would answer the call, and it was only after a trivial incident that had happened on board, known to them both, had been mentioned that he consented to go to the telephone.

"My husband and I at that sitting had some really intimate talk, and when he said he must go my eyes filled with tears.

Although it was pitch-dark and my voice was under perfect control, he exclaimed at once "Don't cry!" My father came at that sitting to my great delight. The bond between us on earth had been very real. He asked after his sisters, using the pet name of one of my aunts who at that time was in physical life, she has come to me many a time since she passed on. He again reminded me of Malta—and mentioned our old Scottish nurse, calling her by her not very common name, Euphemia, and also the pet name by which we had all called her as children.

"Then an uncle whom I have already mentioned, having recognized him by his laugh. He had been a Bishop in South Africa on this plane, and when I asked him if he was surprised at his surroundings when he found himself in the next world, he replied: "Indeed I was!"

"Then came further confirmation. Two days later I received a letter from Admiral Usborne Moore. He was a stranger to me and addressed me as "Madam." He was known as the writer of several books on spiritualism and was a keen investigator. He wrote that at a seance with Mrs. Wriedt a voice had come through claiming to be that of Philip de Crespigny.

"But I never knew you," the Admiral protested.

"Which of the de Crespignys are you? I never knew any of them, but one was in the Navy and married a daughter of Sir Cooper Key."

"That is my wife," was the answer. "I am Philip. I was in the Navy, and I have two brothers still alive," and he gave the names correctly.

"But I did not know you" Admiral Moore went on. "Why have you come to me?"

"Because you knew Sir Cooper Key. He is here."

"When did you pass out?"

"About a year and a half ago."

"The Admiral fancied vaguely he had heard of my husband's death five years previously, and wrote to a mutual friend to inquire. The friend also thought it had been about five years, but the year and a half given by the communicator from the "other side" was correct putting any suggestion of telepathy or the subconscious mind out of court again.

"I had at this time a near relative who wished to verify for herself the experiences of which I spoke. I was anxious she should have something of a convincing nature, so previously to her projected visit I asked my husband to recall some incident that would satisfy her with regard to his identity.

"I asked him to give the pet name by which he had called her. After some hesitation he said he could not quite get it, but it was a short name with three letters in it. This was correct, and he made a further attempt which was almost successful, and interesting as being evidently a genuine effort of memory.

"He told me that as they leave the physical brain to disintegrate with the body, it is uncertain how much they can take over with them of facts stored in the memory. There is also to be considered the readjustment of the vehicle of consciousness necessary before they can tune in to physical conditions, for us on this plane to attempt to arbitrate upon how much or what they ought to remember when returning to communicate, is probably a display of ignorance on our part. My relation obtained the evidence that certainly convinced her at the time, and she said afterwards had robbed her of the fear of death for good and all.

"My husband gave his name and asked if she remembered a ring he had given her many years ago. She was nervous and hesitated, then with an effort of memory asked:

"Do you mean the silver ring you gave me in Bermuda when I was twelve years old?"

"Yes," he replied, "with the crown on it."

"She gasped with astonishment. The ring referred to was of silver beaten out of a shilling by the ships armorer in the days when my father had been C. in C. on the North American Station, leaving the pattern of laurel leaves round it and the crown in the center.

"And you lost it," he went on, "but knew when you lost it." It seemed she had allowed it to be put into a Christmas pudding and had never seen it again. Trivial—but it went home!

"I have heard many languages spoken in Mrs. Wriedt's seance-room, one of special interest, both sides of the conversation being carried on in Hindustani.

"A man known to me, and his wife, had lately returned from India, where he had held an official position, and the latter came with me to a sitting with Mrs. Wriedt at which about ten persons were present. A native landowner known to her and her husband in India spoke to me in a strange language. She was touched by the trumpet, showing the communication was for her, someone suggested she should answer the speaker in Hindustani. This let loose the flow of his eloquence, a torrent of words in a strange tongue was the result, some of which was evidently intelligible to her. The only syllables I could disentangle from the riot of speech were "Bala Khan," which I heard distinctly, and was repeated when he finished up at the top of the scale in a sort of screech which I was told was very characteristic.

"Then Colonel Johnson, who was present, and had himself spent a great part of his life in India, said: "Turn Hindustani bolta?"—I think I have got it right, the other voice shot out:

"Beshakk!"—the question being: "Do you speak Hindustani?" and the answer: "Of course!"

"Dr. Sharp," who controls Mrs. Wriedt's seances from the other side, then came to explain that the old man, Bala Khan, was trying to say how much he loved the family, and added: "You have a daughter."

"She said yes, and the voice then, so strong and powerful, it could have been heard easily throughout the house, went on: "The old man was saying that he was living in the glory of God." "Has he forgiven the man who sent him across?"

"That man was innocent," was the reply.

"Then who was guilty?"

"He will tell you that himself," and later on at another sitting he came again and described the conditions of his own murder, exonerating the relative who had been suspected of it.

"On one occasion after a sitting, when the light was turned up, the trumpet that a moment before had been on the floor in the center of the circle, was hanging by its thin end to the ceiling of the very high room, it hung there sufficiently long for everyone to see it. Then, as the ether was thrown into movement by the sudden influx of light, it fell and hit one of the party a really sharp blow on the shoulder—sharp enough to convince him it could not be put down to his subconscious mind!

"One evening I was sitting alone with a reading-lamp at my left shoulder, when quite suddenly a shadow passed between me and the printed page. It was so unlike an ordinary flicker of the electric current that it caught my attention. There seemed to be something more deliberate about it as though a bat or bird had passed between me and the light. But discovering nothing to account for it, I resumed reading and thought no more about it.

"The following day I was lunching with friends and unexpectedly to me Admiral Usborne Moore—whom I had met and made friends with after his first letter to me—was one of the guests. On meeting me he exclaimed: "I did not know I was to meet you, but apparently the Lady of the Lamp, who I suppose was Miss Nightingale, did, for I was at Mrs. Wriedt's this morning and she asked me to give you a message. It conveys nothing to me but you may be able to understand it."

"T was to tell you it was she who threw the shadow across your book last night."

There we have another instance of a communication that cannot be explained by the subconscious mind.

"At another time the Admiral, before witnesses who can confirm the circumstances, greeted me with: "Have you a son in the Dardanelles?" I hesitated.

"I thought you told me your son was fighting in Egypt," he went on, "but at a seance this morning your husband came through and asked me to tell you not to be anxious about your son in the Dardanelles, as he and others were looking after him."

"My son had been fighting in Egypt, but two days previously I had received the news of his appointment as A.D.G. to General Sir William Birdwood in the Dardanelles, with whom he served afterwards in France until he finally rejoined his regiment in India.

"There seems to be a tendency on the part of newcomers into investigation of this subject to ignore the good evidence and batten on the bad!

Four Voices Speaking Simultaneously
French, German, Croatian, Serbian, Greek, Hindustani ...

"I have heard four voices speaking simultaneously in Mrs. Wriedt's seance-room, one at my ear, purporting to be my husband in a voice audible to everyone present, speaking apparently from the air about my own private affairs, while one at the further side of the circle was speaking in Dutch. At various times thirteen or fourteen different languages have been spoken, Mrs. Wriedt is familiar with no language except her own. These languages have included Breton-French—a very distinctive patois—Hindustani, Croatian, Serbian, Maltese, modern Greek, besides the more ordinary French, German, Swedish and others. There was no fumbling among the sitters for a response, in every case the communicator directly addressed the one person in the circle without any hesitation who understood the language spoken. This in itself is evidential. On occasions when it was an unusual tongue such as Serbian or Croatian there would be present only one person who understood it, and there might be great difficulty in getting through more than a word or so, but sufficient for recognition by the sitter for whom it was intended.

"Dr. Sharpe" the control, would then speak and throw light on the situation. With no direct voice medium have I ever heard so many strange and unusual languages articulated in the seance-room.

"When my father's time as Captain on the North American Station came to an end, he was recalled with some urgency to England with Captain Fisher, as he was then, to take command of an emergency fleet specially mobilized, owing to what was at the time called the Russian 'scare'—though of what the particular scare was about I have no recollection. Whatever it was, it came to nothing, fortunately the situation was cleared up and the fleet waiting for orders at Weymouth was eventually demobilized as rapidly as it had been called into being.

"In Mrs. Wriedt's seance-room on one occasion I was talking to my father, who had passed over more than five-and-twenty years previously, and for some reason I referred to this incident—mainly, I think, as a small test of memory, but on this occasion I was spoken to by him.

"Do you remember," I asked, "taking command of the emergency fleet assembled at Weymouth at the time of the Russian 'scare' in 1879?"

"Of course I do," he answered instantly, "but it was in '78 not '79."

"My memory was at fault, not his. He was perfectly correct, as I found out afterwards. In 1914, when the sitting took place, very few even among naval men would have remembered the Russian 'scare,' which came to nothing, of all those years ago—much less Mrs. Wriedt, but the voice, as objective as yours or mine, corrected me without a moment's hesitation.

"When in Malta as a child, among the friends of my parents I can remember a Captain and Mrs. Morant, the latter was specially impressed on my mind owing to the fact that she gave me my first paint-box—a tin box with real water-colors, very different from the pale substitute generally considered good enough for the early dabbler!I had entirely lost sight of them and had never seen or heard of them since those days of childhood.

At the sitting at which my father first spoke, he was followed by a voice giving the name "Sophie."

"I am sorry," I replied, "I never knew anyone called Sophie."

"Yes, you did—you knew me," was the answer.

"Can you give me your other name—your surname?" and when the name Morant was given I remembered and placed the speaker.

"Your father brought me to speak to you. Do you remember me?"

"Of course I do!" I exclaimed.

"You gave me my first paint-box when we were in Malta. But I didn't know your name was Sophie."

"You probably never heard it. We were friends of your father and mother, and we still are friends over here."

"Have you been over there long?"

"About two years. My husband is still in earth life."

On consulting a book of reference after the sitting, I found the Christian name of the speaker had been Sophia, that she had passed over about two years previously and that her husband was still alive.

"On another occasion the sitter next to me, whom I knew, was the mother of a young lieutenant in the Navy, who had been killed a short time previously in the War. Some engravings of some value had been missing since his death, and as he had been very interested in them his mother was anxious to trace them. When a voice came through giving his name, she explained how they had searched for them everywhere in vain, both in their country and London homes, but the engravings seemed to have entirely disappeared.

"He remembered them perfectly, said he had sent them to be framed, and told her to write to a well-known firm in Portsmouth, giving the name quite clearly, and from whom he felt sure she would get the necessary information. His mother wrote to me later as she thought I should be interested in the subsequent development. She had written to the firm in question asking if they could tell her anything of the missing engravings. The reply was that they remembered them perfectly, but they were no longer in their possession; they had been framed, packed in a case and despatched to their country house in Oxfordshire.

"On receipt of this information another search had been carried out in the house, and finally the missing engravings were discovered inside an unopened packing-case lying among some lumber in an attic. As often happened during the economical days of the War, an old packing-case had been used, which had put the searchers off the scent in the first instance, and they had not taken the trouble to open it. It is difficult in such a case to see where the subconscious mind could have come in, without stretching the point beyond the bounds of probability.

"During the years Mrs. Wriedt was in England the number of my sittings with her must have run certainly into three figures, and I think I may say I could count the blanks upon the fingers of one hand. Her kind-heartedness toward those who mourned was never-failing, she would use her gift for them freely and with a generosity that often left her tired and spent. On the rare occasions when there were no results she refused to take a fee, saying that "if you pay for a pair of boots you have the right to expect to get the boots," and that if she gave nothing she would take nothing.

"Shortly after one of Mrs. Wriedt's visits to England, a newspaper was sent to me anonymously from America. It contained an article headed "Exposure of Mrs. Wriedt."

"The main indictment was that after one of her sittings the writer had detected drops of water adhering to the inner sides of the trumpet, which obviously suggested the condensation of human breath, with the implication that Mrs. Wriedt had been herself speaking through it.[26] As it was her invariable custom to hold the trumpet under the cold water tap between each sitting—an office I had often performed for her— the "exposure" made no more impression upon me than many other "exposures" of the same description, which I hope to consider in a later chapter.

"The evidence for survival of personality bearing the hallmark of characteristics, memory, temperament and so on was given me in such abundance through the channel of Etta Wriedt's mediumship that it is impossible to record more than a mere fraction, and the repetition of instance after instance is apt to become wearisome. It is also a fact that nothing will ever bring conviction with the force of first-hand experience. It is possible to accept what you hear, to acknowledge the probability, the logic, the truth itself on the evidence of others, and to be to that extent convinced. But to believe intellectually is not to realize, and realization in its full sense comes only with personal experience, an iota of which is of more value than all the arguments in the world. And it is through the little everyday references to life, the trivial happenings, that conviction comes.

"My husband's grandfather, on his mother's side, Sir John Tyrell, came to speak to me at a séance, I had never known him in earth life and it greatly surprised me that he should wish to communicate. He had been very autocratic in earth life. A few years ago his family place was bought by Mr. Henry Ford, to be near his works at Dagenham, and had the sale taken place before my interview, I have no doubt he would have had something to say on the subject!

---

[26] Yet another unfounded, imbecilic statement.

"He spoke on several matters not only connected with the family, but gave some information about his own development since passing over. He also made one or two allusions to matters I was not clear about.

"At my next sitting, his daughter, my husband's mother, came through to explain, and solved some confusion I felt as to her identity by describing herself as the "Dowager," she referred in detail to family dissensions and their consequences, about which the medium could have known nothing, and of which I knew very little, as it had all happened before I married into the family. No subconscious mind could be reasonably held accountable for such results, nor for the strong objective voices audible to everyone present."

"I went to Mrs Wriedt's sittings in a somewhat sceptical spirit, but I came to the conclusion that she is a genuine and remarkable psychic and has given abundant proof to others beside myself that the voices and the contents of the messages are wholly beyond the range of trickery or collusion. I am convinced of the genuineness of the phenomena."

–SIR WILLIAM BARRETT

SIR WILLIAM BARRETT[27]
ON THE THRESHOLD OF THE UNSEEN
1912

William F. Barrett (1844 1925) was a British physicist and a leading figure in the early years of psychical research, investigating telepathy and clairvoyance, apparitions, mediumship, dowsing, deathbed visions of deceased persons, and related topics. Barrett co-founded both the Society for Psychical Research and the American Society for Psychical Research (Ed.).

---

[27] Sir William Fletcher Barrett (10 February 1844 in Kingston, Jamaica – 26 May 1925) was an English parapsychologist; Professor of Physics at The University of Dublin, President and one of the founders of The Society of Psychical Research. See: *On The Threshold of The Unseen*, E. P. Dutton, 1919.

"When, after examination of the room, Mrs. Wriedt and Miss Ramsden entered, the door was locked, and one of the electric lights over our head was left on to illuminate the room. We sat on chairs adjoining each other, I sat next to Mrs. Wriedt, and held her hand. Miss Ramsden sat on my left. We asked Mrs. Wriedt to let us try in the light first, and at her suggestion Miss R. held the small end of a large aluminum trumpet to her car; the larger end I supported with my left hand. My body, therefore, came between the trumpet and the medium. I had previously looked into the trumpet, which was perfectly bare and smooth. Presently Miss Ramsden said she heard a voice speaking to her, and entered into conversation with the voice. I only heard a faint whispering sound, but no articulate words.

"To avoid the possibility of Mrs. Wriedt being the source of the whispering, I engaged her in talk, and while she was speaking Miss Ramsden still heard the faint voice in the trumpet, but begged us to stop speaking, as it prevented her hearing distinctly what the voice said. Miss Ramsden assured me afterwards there could be no doubt whatever that the voice in the trumpet was independent of Mrs. Wriedt, and I can testify that I watched the medium and saw nothing suspicious in the movement of her lips. She did not move from her place, and no accomplice or concealed arrangement could possibly have produced the voice.

"As I did not hear what the voice said, I have asked Miss Ramsden to add a few lines."

Note By Miss Ramsden

"The speaker claimed to be the bearer of a message from one of my relations who has died; he told me that, contrary to my expectations, I should receive a visit from a person who was named. This was fulfilled on the following Monday. Here I must add that if this is explained by thought transference, we must suppose it possible for Mrs. Wriedt to receive telepathic communications from people of whose existence she knows nothing, in this case the person was in a foreign, country. While holding the trumpet I could feel the vibration of the little voice inside.

"When the voice ceased speaking, the trumpet was placed with its broad end on the floor, standing upright, near Miss Ramsden. The electric light was now switched off, and the room became absolutely dark. A very loud man's voice almost immediately called out: "God bless you, God bless you." Mrs. Wriedt said it was the soi disant[28] 'John King.'[29] I begged her to place her right hand on mine, which held her left hand. She did so, and I distinctly felt the two hands, my left hand being free.

"During every seance with her, Mrs. Wriedt remained perfectly normal, talking with me or others present, and not in the least excited. On this occasion, in a few moments, I felt something rather cold gently stroking my face, and as at a previous sitting when a rose was placed in my hand, the act was performed without any fumbling about. This was very curious, as the room was so dark that nothing whatever could be seen. I went to Mrs. Wriedt's séances in a somewhat skeptical spirit, but I came to the conclusion that she is a genuine and remarkable medium, and has given abundant proof to others besides myself that the voices and the contents of the messages given are wholly beyond the range of trickery or collusion."

---

[28] Soi Distant: Self Styled. A perfect description of the spirit John King.

[29] John King, the most romantic spirit control. He claims to have been Henry Owen Morgan, the buccaneer, who was knighted by Charles II. And was appointed Governor of Jamaica. He first appeared with the Davenport Brothers in 1850, and was first seen in the flash of a pistol fired by Ira Davenport in the dark. He remained as spirit manager with the Davenports throughout their career and in typtology (The science or theory of the rapping sounds produced by spirits at a séance-Ed), or direct voice gave them sound advice in difficult positions. His activity was multifarious. While faithfully serving the Davenport Brothers he took charge of the performances in the Koon loghouse in the wilds of Ohio. Here he assumed an august mien. As the head of a band of 160 spirits he claimed descent from a race of men known by the generic title Adam, and having as leaders " the most ancient angels. " They signed their communications as King No. 1, No. 2., etc., and sometimes: Servant and Scholar of God. In his last incarnation he strayed from the path of virtue and became a redoubtable pirate. He communicated in direct voice through a trumpet, his own invention, and through direct writing. See: *Wizards of The North, The Brothers Davenport, The World Renowned Spiritual Mediums*, by N. Riley Heagerty, 2019.

THE EVIDENCE OF THE DIRECT VOICE:
THE RETURN OF W.T. STEAD
1909

"This was the first real personal evidence of survival he had encountered in his twenty years of investigation." ~ Charles Tweedale referring to W. Wortley Baggally's outstanding experience with Mrs. Wriedt

The Reverend Charles Tweedale: Man's Survival After Death

"These are the accounts of my own sittings with Mrs. Wriedt. In 1912, the year of Mrs. Wriedt's first visit, I had four sittings. At the first, on 31st May, Mr. Stead greeted me in a loud voice, clear and unmistakable, bidding me welcome to his house. Many other very evidential things came for the other sitters, including the etherialization of a man who had shot himself, and who was identified by one of the sitters, but beyond a voice giving the name " William," I got nothing more on this occasion (cf. 248). On Monday, 3rd June, I had the most remarkable sitting of the series. I had written for W. Wortley Baggally, Esq., one of the Council of the S.P.R., to join me, and he did so on this evening, therefore I asked permission to introduce a friend, which was granted. In order to make things more evidential he was introduced under the name Wortley, one of his Christian names.

"There were about seven persons present in addition to myself, my wife and Mr. W. Wortley Baggally, all strangers to us. Mr. Wortley sat next to Mrs. Wriedt in the place of honor. After we had examined the room the light was put out, the door locked, and we sat in darkness. The musical polyphone now played, most beautifully, Schubert's Ave Maria, and we then sang. Very soon water was sprinkled on us and a deep and solemn voice spoke, giving us a benediction. My wife now saw a form standing near where Mr. Wortley was. Mrs. Wriedt said that there was a man with a beard near him. Then Mrs. Wriedt said: "I get two names for you, James and William. Did you know anyone with these names?"

"Mr. Wortley said he did. Mr. Baggally informed us after the sitting that James and William were the two names especially connected with his family which had been used for generations. He was called William and his brother was named James. Now a George Wallace came for a Miss Wallace sitting next to me. She recognized her brother by his voice and what was told her. She wept softly for a long time afterwards. We now saw a luminous star and Mrs. Wriedt said she saw a spirit who gave the name of Perrine. Mr. Wortley said that he had known some one of that name.

"Other voices came to the other sitters, then a voice to my wife, giving the name "Frank Woodward." My wife was astonished at this and asked who he was. The voice replied that she was the daughter of Frank Burnett and that he knew her when she was at School. I had never heard his name before and did not know my wife had attended this school. [My wife after the sitting informed me that she knew Frank Woodward seventeen years before and had not seen him since. He was her schoolmaster at School. She did not know that he was dead, but on writing her mother on our return home she found that he had died more than a year before the date of this sitting.] Immediately after this there began a most remarkably loud and lively whistling. It went on for some time and then Mrs. Wriedt said: "Did you know anyone who whistled like that, Mr. Wortley?"

"Mr. Wortley at first temporized and said he would like something more evidential than the whistling, but every time he asked for speech, or something more, the whistling burst out louder than ever, and was evidently teasing him, and this became so manifest that the whole of the company present laughed heartily at the answering whistling. Then came a voice: "Wake up, Wortley." Mr. Wortley replied that he was very much awake. The vigorous whistling now ceased, and suddenly a man's deep voice sang, most beautifully, *Rocked in the Cradle of the Deep.* Mrs. Wriedt asked whether Mr. Wortley knew anyone who used to sing that song. He replied: "Yes, a dear friend whom I knew." The deep voice here chimed in: "I should just think you did, old man." Then *Auld Lang Syne* was splendidly sung by the same deep voice, and Mr. Wortley said it was very appropriate.

"Almost immediately afterwards a woman's voice sang exquisitely When Other Lips *and Other Hearts.* When the song was finished the same deep voice that had rendered *Rocked in the Cradle of the Deep* and *Auld Lang Syne* cried out: "Now do you know her?" with great emphasis on the last word. This marvelous manifestation, which was the great feature of the evening, then ceased. Every word was distinctly heard by all present. [The full significance of this was not apparent until my wife and I received Mr. W. Wortley Baggally's explanation after the sitting, then the wonder of it all became apparent. He informed us that his father was a remarkable whistler and used to whistle in an exactly similar way, also that the song, *Rocked in the Cradle of the Deep*, was his father's favorite song and the one he was particularly known by. He also informed us that he recognized the identity of the lady, a very dear friend who used to sing to him the same song, *When Other Lips and Other Hearts*.

"He was deeply impressed, and told us that this was the first real personal evidence of survival that he had encountered in his twenty years of investigation. We are certain that Mr. W. Wortley Baggally's identity was not known on this occasion to anyone present save ourselves, and we knew absolutely nothing of Mr. Baggally's private or family affairs, or of the names and incidents connected with him which transpired at this sitting.] No sooner had this wonderful piece of evidence ceased than a voice came for my wife, giving the name of Mrs. Wood. At this we were greatly surprised. She was an old parishioner of mine whom I had found dead in her chair by her fireside, on the morning of 25th September 1911.

"On the table by her side there was a pot of water and a candle stick. We asked her how she died. She replied: "I began to be very drowsy, very drowsy. I could not keep my eyes open. I then drank a glass of water and I remembered no more until I woke up in heaven." This was so pathetic that all present exclaimed at it. She now conversed with my wife on very evidential and private matters known only to ourselves. I then put a test question about the tombstone over her grave. It had been most negligently allowed to lie prostrate on the ground for several months until my strong representations had secured its restoration.

"Thinking this would be a test, I said: "Can you tell me something about your grave?" She replied, to my disappointment: "Do you mean about it caving in?" I had never heard of her grave caving in.

She immediately added: "I think it is better not to let them rest in Weston churchyard but to cremate them." We could not understand this at all, but it turned out to be a splendid test, one that utterly destroys the telepathic and subliminal theories of these communications, for the information conveyed was (1) unknown to me, (2) contrary to my strong preconception—on which at that moment I was concentrating, while the reference to cremation puzzled us completely. Five days after this sitting we returned home. Immediately on alighting upon the platform we were told that my patron, the squire of the parish, was dead, and that they were going to cremate him, and not bury the body in the church. We heard both facts then for the first time. Next day I saw my sexton and asked him whether Mrs. Wood's grave had ever caved in. He at once replied: " Yes, sir, didn't you know? I spent all one afternoon setting it right. " My patron died on 6th June, this message re cremation being thus received three days before his death, of which we did not hear until the 8th. After several other voices and a talk with the loud, cheery voice of John King, my father's name was given and the voice addressed me.

He said: "Do you remember Dr. Hoyle?"

I replied with another question. "How did he pass over?"

The answer was: "He was killed by a blow on the head."

I thought this wrong at the time. The spirit then touched my wife on her chin, cheek, and hand, saying: "How do you do, my daughter-in-law?"

While this voice was speaking to my wife, Mrs. C. Stewart, of Cupar Angus[30] who was present, had the voice of her son whispering in her ear. She told us that she recognized his voice and also the correctness of what he told her. The reply of my father touching the death of Dr. Hoyle was, I thought, erroneous. I had always understood that he was drowned. He was my father's assistant.

"One morning, some little time after leaving my father's employ, he fell ill, and in delirium got out of his bedroom window early in the morning and ran up the deserted street until he came to the river. Here he tried to cross a dam or weir but, slipping, was precipitated down a steep slope of about fifteen feet into a pool of water, where he was drowned, so I always understood. On returning home from this sitting I went on to Lancashire, and there visited my mother, to obtain the true particulars.

I said: " He was drowned, was he not?

"She replied: " No, he had a great wound in his head, didn't you know? He hit his head against an iron spike as he fell down the slope of the dam."

"I was entirely ignorant of this, and had been all ray [sic] life, thinking that his death was due to drowning only. [Here again the subliminal theory is completely shattered.] This was a singularly evidential sitting, and most impressive.

In 1913 I had three sittings. At the one on 16th June a voice came for my wife, saying: "It's Grannie."

My wife suggested names. Voice: "No. No."

Wife. Who, then? Voice: "Grannie Burnett."

What? Father's mother, Voice: "Yes. Yes." Have you a message for us?

Voice: "Yes. Mary is here." Who is Mary? (Here my wife suggested several Marys.) Voice (impatiently): "No. No. No."

---

[30] Coupar Angus is a town in Perth and Kinross, Scotland.

Wife. "Can you tell us your Christian name?"

No reply, but a few seconds later Mrs. Wriedt said: "She says it was Catharine." This was correct. During the evening my wife remembered that her grandmother, whom she never saw, had adopted a girl named Mary and that she had died about three years previously under rather peculiar circumstances. On going home some weeks later my wife told this to her father, who was much impressed and informed her that the girl Mary had been buried in the same grave as Grannie Burnett, and that the impatient " No. No. No, " was one of her characteristic expressions. This was unknown to myself and wife, and Mrs. Wriedt could have no possible knowledge of it. During this sitting Mrs. Wriedt said that she saw a little girl, with very light hair, elevated above the floor, and that she came for us. My wife could not see her.

"At the sitting of 18th June one of the sitters (who was not present on 16th June and who was an entire stranger to us) suddenly turned to my wife and said: " There is a beautiful little girl with very fair hair standing close to you. Do you see her?" My wife did not, nor did I. Returning home on 20th June we were in the long underground passage at King's Cross Station. Suddenly my wife cried out: "See the girl." The little fair-headed girl appeared to her walking just behind the porter who was carrying our luggage, and after accompanying us about fifty yards vanished when at the top of the steps and about two yards into the sunshine.

"On Saturday, 21st June, I was reading the newspaper in the breakfast-room alone and with the door shut. Suddenly I caught a glimpse of someone close to me stooping down behind my paper. It was so realistic that it made me start violently. I thought it was one of my children. I at once rose from my seat and looked under the table for the child. Finding no one there, I searched the small room, but excepting myself there was no mortal in it. During this search the door was shut (it has no keyhole), the blinds and curtains were drawn, and I did not speak. I was just about to settle down again to the paper, under the impression that 1must have been mistaken, when the door opened and my wife took a step forward into the room. Before I could utter a single word, she exclaimed: " Oh, Charles, see the little girl! " She saw her distinctly standing near me, the vision lasting for several minutes.

"I now told my wife what I had seen and she questioned the little girl. The reply (heard clairaudiently) was that she had just allowed me to get a glimpse of her. On looking up my records I find that the same little girl has been seen by our servant on 26th March 1912 and, a few days after, by my wife, both in daylight, also by my daughter Marjorie on 19th March 1913, again in broad daylight. My daughter took notice of the flaxen hair, remarking that it was almost white. No details of these appearances had previously been published. All who have seen her describe her as a beautiful little girl of about six years of age. It will thus be seen that the figure seen and described by Mrs. Wriedt on 16th June has been observed by at least five other persons under circumstances precluding all possibility of hallucination or fraud."

"Come we now more particularly to the manifestations of Mr. W. T. Stead after his passing in the Titanic disaster. Previous to his ill-fated voyage, Mr. Stead had written me to the effect that he was going to the United States[31] and proposed bringing Mrs. Wriedt back with him, and we agreed to meet at his home in Wimbledon on his return. Bearing this in mind there is little doubt but that we had indications of the approach and completion of the tragedy. At any rate this is what occurred. On 8th April 1912 we all retired about 11 p.m., and some little time after, when they were in bed, our two servants, Ida and Martha, who were in the big nursery with the children, heard a loud crying, sobbing and wailing proceeding from the passage and landing outside the nursery door. They described it as like people in great trouble and distress. It went on for ten minutes or more, and then ceased. The girl Martha had only just come, and knew nothing about our psychic experiences, we being careful not to tell new-comers anything about them. I questioned both girls closely, especially the new one, but could not shake their testimony. And they afterwards affirmed the same on oath. The Titanic sailed from Southampton on April 10th. The next entry in my journal is under date Monday, 15th April 1912, as follows:— About 11.30 wife came running to me in alarm (children and servants had gone to bed) saying that a man with thick eyebrows and a beard under his chin and round his face had passed through the kitchen where she was. He had on a greyish or mixture tweed suit, with a short, round library coat. Shortly after this, while in the kitchen, she heard wailing, crying sounds, and a kind of moaning. It sounded like many people in great trouble, and was loud, seeming to be in the house, but she could not locate it definitely. She heard it both in the kitchen and

[31] Stead was going to New York City to give a lecture on world peace at Carnegie Hall and planned on bringing Mrs. Wriedt back with him to his home in Wimbledon and to Julia's Bureau, a public institution founded by Stead in 1909 for free communication with the afterlife.

in the passage. At this time we were all in absolute ignorance of the Titanic disaster and did not hear the news until the following morning. On 16th April I enter in my journal: Just heard of dreadful disaster to the *Titanic* and feared loss of nearly 2000 lives. Mr. Stead is reported lost. I sincerely hope this is not the case, as I have arranged to be at his house, with Mrs. Wriedt, at the end of May. Alas! it was only too true, and soon the news of the awful tragedy, with all its poignant details of heroism and suffering, thrilled the civilized world.

"The *Titanic* struck the iceberg at 11.35 p.m. on April 14th, and sank at 2.20 a.m. on the morning of the 15th. The maids heard the wailing and crying, probably about 11.30 p.m. on the 8th. My wife heard the wailing and crying and saw the apparition about 11.30 p.m. on the 15th. Afterward, when shown a photo of Mr. Stead, my wife said that the apparition she saw bore a strong resemblance to him, and the description of his appearance and dress was characteristic of him. Survivors say that as the ship went down "There fell on our ears the most appalling noise that human beings ever heard. A great chorus of human agony, a great and bitter cry went wailing up to the black dome of night, as 1600 human beings were plunged into the sea of death. It was nothing but a great weltering mass of drowning people, all struggling. The sounds rent our hearts. Terrible shrieks and a chorus of groans arose for an hour. We only thought of rowing harder to escape those haunting death cries which wrung our very souls. The cries of anguish of the unhappy passengers redoubled, sounding like the singing of a great dirge by a very large choir. A forecast of these cries would seem to have been first simulated to us, as a note of impending doom, just before the great ship put out on her fateful voyage, and then repeated a few hours after its tragic ending."

"Mr. Stead manifesting to us probably in view of my agreement to meet him at his house on his return, while it is remarkable that both manifestations took place at the same hour of the night (about 11.30) as that in which the great vessel received the fatal stroke. Ships that pass in the night, and speak to each other in passing, only a signal is shown and a distant voice in the darkness, so on the ocean of life we pass and speak to one another, only a look and a voice, then darkness again, and a silence. Mr. Stead, when last seen on the ship by the occupants of the last boat to push off—stood alone at the edge of the deck in silence, and what seemed to me a prayerful attitude, or one of profound meditation. My last glimpse of the *Titanic* showed him still standing in the same attitude and place.

*"It was the most painful and at the same time the most realistic,
convincing conversation I have ever heard during my investigation."*
–VICE ADMIRAL W. USBORNE MOORE

"On 31st May, at Wimbledon, Mr. Stead addressed me by name in his
vigorous, well-known, characteristic voice, welcoming me to his house!
The voice was loud, clear, distinct and unmistakable. The evidence
for the return of W. T. Stead is of the most positive kind. His first
appearance was to Mrs. Wriedt and her host on 17th April 1912, in
New York, just three days after his passing. On 6th May, immediately
after Mrs. Wriedt's arrival in England, he was both seen and heard at
Wimbledon, first by Admiral Moore at 10.30 a.m. and in the evening
by his daughter, Miss Estelle Stead, as reported in Light of 18th May
and also in Nash's Magazine for July, 1912. In the evening there were
several witnesses present, and the Admiral writes (The Voices, page 19):
"At least forty minutes were taken up by Stead talking to his daughter.
I could not help hearing every word. It was the most painful and at the
same time the most realistic, convincing conversation I have ever heard
during my investigations. The first time he came it was to give directions
to his daughter for the disposal of his private papers. Miss Estelle was
naturally much agitated, and her grief at last reacted upon her father,
who uttered a loud shout: "O my God!" and the manifestation ended.
With reference to this Miss Estelle Stead writes me, under date 3rd
June 1918: "Yes, Admiral Moore's account of my father's conversation
with me, with regard to his affairs, is quite correct," signed, E. W. Stead.

"About ten days after the foundering of the monster ship I held a
small and carefully selected sitting at my house. Mr. Stead's private
secretary was among the sitters. We had hardly commenced when a
voice, which apparently came from behind my right shoulder, exclaimed:
"I am so happy to be with you again." The voice was unmistakably that of
Stead, who immediately began to tell us the events of the dire moments
when the leviathan settled down. There was a short, sharp struggle to
gain his breath and immediately afterwards he came to his senses in
another stage of existence. He was surrounded by hundreds of beings
who, like himself had passed over to the bourne.[32] Stead then had a
long conversation with his secretary. Asked by me if he would show
himself to us, he replied: "Not to-night, but if you go to Cambridge
House I will do so."

---

[32] Bourne: a limit or boundary. In this case, meaning the afterlife.

"I went to Cambridge House and, as he had promised, Stead appeared twice. He was dressed in his usual attire, so familiar to all his friends, and looked supremely happy. After this Mrs. Wriedt sat twice at my house. At the first sitting was a lady who had had no experience and begged me to let her attend in the hope of getting communication with her lost one. At first voices came assuring us that his passing, contrary to rumor, was accidental. A few minutes later the voice of the young man himself—unmistakable to his mother, for such the lady was— was heard, and son and mother had a long conversation, heard by all of us, during which he expressed his wishes concerning the completion of a book, of which no one present knew anything save the mother. The circumstances of the communication were beautiful and touching in the extreme, and I am sure there was not a dry eye in the room. Let scorners and scoffers contemplate this case, and the most callous of them will not mock at the bereaved mother and the comfort that this communion with her beloved son brought to her wounded heart. On the second occasion I sat alone with Mrs. Wriedt. Many of those " I have lost awhile " spoke to me, and John King and others gave me very strong advice which cast serious reflections on one I thoroughly believed in and trusted. What he impressed upon me turned out absolutely true. Had I followed his advice I should have been saved from infinite trouble and disillusion later. I can bear the strongest possible testimony to the psychic power, perfect honesty and good faith of Mrs. Wriedt."

COUNT CHEDO MIYATOVICH
WIMBLEDON, ENGLAND
W.T STEAD RETURNS AGAIN
MAY 16th, 1912

"The most wonderful experience of my life....the almost heavenly joy of hearing the words of my dear mother in our own tongue."
~ Count Chedo Myatovich

Count Chedo Myatovich

"By profession I am a diplomatist, having represented my country, Servia, at the Court of the King of Romania, at the Sublime Porte, three times at the Court of Queen Victoria, and once at the Court of King Edward VII. I am a member of several learned societies on the Continent and in London. I mention these personal facts to show that I am a man accustomed to weigh facts and words in full consciousness of my responsibility. Having heard that the remarkable psychic Mrs. Wriedt was at Wimbledon I arranged for an appointment at 10.30 a.m. on May 16th, 1912. I went there accompanied by my friend Dr. Hinkovitch, a distinguished barrister of Agram, just arrived in London. I and Dr Hinkovitch sat near each other.

"Mrs. Wriedt sat on a chair near me. She started a musical clock and put all the lights out. When a beautiful melody of a sacred character was finished Mrs. Wriedt said that we should be able not only to hear but also to see some spirit friends. "Yes," she continued, "here is the spirit of a young woman. She nods to you, Mr. Miyatovich, do you not see her?" I did not, but my friend saw an oblong piece of illuminated mist.

"She whispers to me," continued Mrs. Wriedt, "that her name is Mayell. Adela or Ada Mayell."

I was astounded. Only three weeks before died Miss Ada Mayell, a very dear friend of mine, to whom I was deeply attached. The next moment a light appeared from behind Mrs. Wriedt and moved from left to right. There in that slowly moving light was, not the spirit, but the very person of my friend William T. Stead, not wrapped in white, but in his usual walking costume.

"Both I and Mrs. Wriedt exclaimed loudly for joy. Hinkovitch, who knew Stead only from photos, said: "Yes, that is Mr Stead." Mr. Stead nodded to me and disappeared. Half-a-minute later he appeared again, looking at me and bowing, again he appeared, and was seen by all three of us more clearly than before. Then we all three distinctly heard these words: "Yes, I am Stead. William T. Stead. My dear friend Miyatovich, I came here expressly to give you fresh proof that there is life after death. You always hesitated to accept that truth." I interrupted him, saying, 'But you know I always believed what you said to me!'

"Yes," he continued, "you believed because I was telling you something about it, now I come here to bring you proof, that you should not only believe but know (pronouncing this word with great emphasis) that there really is a life after death. Here is Adela Mayell, who wishes to speak to you."

"Stead never knew Miss Ada Mayell in life, nor had he ever heard her name before. She then spoke to me in her affectionate and generous manner, trying to reassure me on certain questions which had sadly preoccupied my mind since her death. Mrs. Wriedt and Hinkovitch heard every word. Then, to my own and my Croatian friend's astonishment, a loud voice began to talk to him in the Croatian language. It was an old friend, a physician by profession, who died suddenly from heart disease. They continued for some time the conversation in their native tongue, of which I heard and understood every word. Mrs. Wriedt, for the first time in her life, heard how the Croatian language sounds. I and my Croatian friend were deeply impressed by what we witnessed that day, May 6th.

"I spoke of it to my friends as the most wonderful experience of my life. I spoke of it to the most scientific woman of Germany, Frau Professor Margarette Selenka, who had just returned from Teneriffe. Madame Selenka arrived in London to hear all the details of the Titanic catastrophe, in which her friend Stead perished. By arrangement with Mrs. Wriedt, I and Madame Selenka had a sitting at 8 p. m. on May 24th. After a short time from the beginning of the sitting we all saw Mr. Stead appear, but hardly for more than ten seconds. He reappeared again more clearly, but not so clear as on May 16th. Stead had a long conversation with Madame Selenka and a short one with me. Then Miss Ada Mayell spoke to me. After her my own mother came and spoke to me in our own Servian language most affectionately. Madame Selenka had a very affecting conversation with her late husband, Professor Lorentz Selenka of the Munich University, and also with her own mother, who died last year in Hamburg.

"A friend of Madame Selenka came singing a German song and asked her to join him as they used to do in old times, and Madame Selenka did join him singing. I wish to state publicly that I am deeply grateful to the wonderful gift of Mrs. Wriedt for having enabled me to obtain from my unforgettable friend, W. T. Stead, a convincing proof that there is a life after death, and for having given me the almost heavenly joy of hearing the affectionate words of my dear mother in our own tongue and in getting another and sacred proof of the continuance of the living individuality of one of the most charming, selfless and generous persons whom I have ever known in my life."

Count Chedo Myatovich,
Royal Societies Club, St. James's, London, S.W

REV. CHARLES TWEEDALE
VOICES IN FULL & PARTIAL LIGHT
WITH MRS. WRIEDT

"Does the orthodox reader—the inexperienced—cry impossible?
"It may be necessary here to explain a few points with reference to these direct-voice and other phenomena manifested in the presence of Mrs. Wriedt. Firstly be it noted that the voice can be heard in broad daylight in her presence as well as in the dark, but that it is not so loud, free or continuous. Once it has been established that the voice can be heard in daylight, and under test conditions, the sitters prefer to sit in darkness, owing to the better results obtained, and also to the fact that lights, etherializations, or materializations of the communicating personalities which would be difficult and of rare occurrence in full light are thus frequently seen. *I have had the direct voice absolutely shouting in my own house in daylight* in the presence of myself and several witnesses, also we have had repeated etherializations and materializations in broad daylight and strong lamplight. This shows the presence of very great psychic power. In our case, however, it has always been of rare occurrence, spontaneous, and never under control. With Mrs. Wriedt and other powerful psychics the manifestation, while not so strong in daylight, is under control, almost constantly available, and splendidly evidential. Several investigators have testified to the fact that the voice is heard in Mrs. Wriedt's presence both in gaslight and daylight.

On this note, Admiral Usborne has written in *The Voices,* "Tried first in gaslight, putting the small end of the trumpet to my ear. There were undoubtedly voices in the tube, but I could only catch the names, "William Roger Drake" and "Mary Ella."

January, 11th, 1911 (Moore.)

"First I tried the trumpet in full light, putting the small end to my left ear and balancing the end on the back of a chair. Mrs Wriedt sat close to me on my right. I heard the voices of Iola and Dr. Sharp quite satisfactorily.

"This report by Moore was in broad daylight. In the visit of Mrs. Wriedt to this country during 1912-1913 many persons made the test of hearing the voices in the light, Mr. William Jeffrey of Glasgow hearing them both in daylight and electric light. Sir Oliver Lodge informs me, under date 14th August 1920, that he has heard the voice in the trumpet when held to his ear, in the presence of Mrs. Wriedt, in daylight, the voice being faint and in whispers. He also adds: " I know that Mrs. Wriedt is genuine."

"Under date 19th August 1920 Mrs K. Kennedy of 46 Chepstow Place, W.2, writes that she has heard the voice in the trumpet in a room well lit with the electric light, Mrs Wriedt sitting at the other end of it. The voice was faint. Mr. Kennedy also adds that he has heard the voice in the trumpet in the electric light at the same time that Mrs. Wriedt and Mrs. Kennedy have been talking together in the room. Sir A. Conan Doyle has also heard the voice distinctly in broad daylight. That the voices are produced in the trumpet in brilliant light by normally invisible personalities, other than and distinct from Mrs. Wriedt, is proved beyond the possibility of a doubt. These voices are heard both directly without the aid of a trumpet, and also through an aluminum trumpet, which is used for the purpose of magnifying their volume, many of them being faint. The trumpet often alters the tone or timbre of the voice, and when the tone of the voice is not recognized this is generally the cause. The disguising effect of a speaking trumpet or megaphone upon the human voice is well known. I have heard the spirit voice of my father so absolutely exact in tone as to thrill me through and through. Tonal individuality of voice is one of those things practically impossible to effectively imitate, even if the psychic had known the person in earth life, which is almost invariably not the case.

"Very often, however, these voices come entirely independent of the trumpet, sometimes whispering in one's ear, at others of such remarkable power, depth and volume as to make the room resound again. Often the voice will be sounding loudly in the room, either through or without the trumpet, and at the same time two or three of the sitters will have voices whispering in their ears and conversing on intimate and private family matters.

Frequently, two or more voices are heard speaking loudly at the same time and often the voice is heard speaking at the same time that Mrs. Wriedt is conversing or explaining matters."

"As the result of my own experience of the whole range of the phenomena, 1 can unhesitatingly confirm the vast testimony of Admiral Moore, and can speak with the same emphasis. It has been said by those who have had little personal experience of these things, and have not fully weighed the evidence, that all the information is obtained from our subliminal self (this theory is a very useful one to cover ignorance or lack of experience). It is blown to atoms by the facts (1) that information is very often imparted of which one never had any previous knowledge, (2) that information and advice are often given which are distasteful to and absolutely against the judgment and settled opinion of the investigator (cf. Voices, page 14), (3) that future events are accurately foretold.

Man's Survival After Death, has an astonishing story attached to it. I had ordered a rare copy of the book in the 1990's from an antiquarian, metaphysical book dealer in Michigan. After a few weeks and the book not having arrived, I contacted UPS to see what was up. They looked at the tracking information and said that, unfortunately, the book had been lost. The book was an expensive, rare find, published in 1909 and it was discouraging to hear the bad news. I contacted the *same* book dealer again and asked him if he could try to find me *another* copy. A few weeks passed and one day I noticed a book had been delivered and was sitting on my porch in its padded envelope. Upon opening it I saw that it was from the same dealer, no bill attached. The label indicated that it was postmarked only the week before. Upon opening it I immediately saw that the book had been engraved by the author, Charles Tweedale, to none other than the American direct voice medium, Etta Wriedt. *I was holding in my hands the very book owned by Etta.* It is, as you can imagine, a priceless treasure sitting in my library. Etta passed away in Detroit, in 1942, and after fifty years, the inscribed book, *somehow,* then made its way to that rare book dealer, then *somehow* made its way to me in of all places, the very birthplace of Etta, Oswego, New York. So, the first book had to be lost in order for me to have acquired the second, inscribed book.

I wonder if Etta had something to do with that? I choose to believe, yes (Ed.).

JAMES COATES
HAS W.T. STEAD RETURNED?

Cambridge House, Wimbledon, England, 1912

There are additional testimonies I have also included below concerning Mr. Stead documented by Coates including Steads loyal secretary, Edith

Harper, Serocold Skeels and Estelle Stead, Colonel E. R. Johnson and Julia's Bureau members.

Wednesday, May 15th
Julia's Circle

"There was one stranger present, a physician much interested in psychic research. ... As usual, the phenomena began very quickly and continued throughout the seance with but few gaps. Mr. Stead spoke. He welcomed the doctor to the circle, and greeted me and other members. An Indian came and told Mrs. Wriedt that her husband in Detroit, Michigan, had slipped on the outer steps leading up to the house and sprained his ankle. (A letter received later confirmed this).

"Wednesday, May 29th. William Stead, junr., who passed over several years before his father, came and talked with his sister, who told him she recognized his voice the same as she had last year. I can support Miss Estelle in this statement. There are a few spirit voices I have noticed which never alter, and one is young Stead's. I have often talked to him; the voice and who talked to them for several minutes. The lady on my left got into touch with young Brailey, who was drowned in the *Titanic*. Julia manifested and greeted Miss Estelle Stead and all the members of the circle."

Wednesday, June 19th

"The members of 'Julia's Circle ' assembled in the drawing-room, where they examined a photograph taken that day in the seance-room in the dark by a lady. The picture is undoubtedly of psychic origin. It shows the cabin with door open and apparently broken, a port-hole, ropes hanging about, a face which is very like W. T. Stead. We then went upstairs to the seance room. The psychic switched off the lights, and before she had time to regain her chair, 'Dr. Sharp's' voice was heard. He greeted the sitters by name and carried on a brief conversation in a clear voice with three of them. Iola spoke to me, and afterwards greeted the sitters with a little speech. She was instantly followed by Mr. Stead, who spoke rapidly to his daughter on private matters, and then said, with reference to a narrative on his life, which was to be written by his private secretary:

"I want to get right on. I want Edith to write it as I want it."

A sitter, "he is in a hurry."

W. T. Stead: "Did you ever know me to take my time over anything?"

There was a chorus of "No!" from all present.

W. T. Stead: "How are you, Admiral?"

Admiral Moore: "Delighted to hear you again."

A few final words to his daughter followed.

Admiral Moore: "Will you tell us about the photograph?"

W. T. Stead: "The photograph represents what took place in the *Titanic*, as near as I can give it you."

Admiral Moore: "Is that your cabin door?"

W. T. Stead: "Yes, and the port-hole."

Julia now manifested, as usual, to close the seance, and talked in eulogistic terms of Mr. Stead. While she was speaking, there was a shout, "Stained glass, Julia." The last utterance of Mr. Stead was—to me—the most striking evidential fact of the seance. He was, in life, surrounded by a knot of women who adored him for his kindly sympathy. When one of them approached him with some complimentary speech he would good naturedly turn it off by saying "Stained glass."

Wednesday, July 3rd

"Directly the lights were out, 'Dr. Sharp,' gave a general greeting to the sitters, then a great number of spirit lights, a flash of light on the ceiling of the room, and a partial etherealization were seen. There was an illumined head and some white stuff underneath, but the features were not distinguishable. Then a voice, "Iola, that was Mr. Stead." Many spirits manifested to their friends. W. Stead spoke for a long time with his sister Estelle. I asked him to give my kindest regards to his father. He replied, "He hears you, Admiral."

"I am not justified in revealing the hundred private details which came out and gave conviction to individual sitters. But these notes may be sufficient to confirm the reiterated statements of all serious investigators during the last forty years that the best results can only be achieved by the circle being composed of the same people, sitting on the same day of the week at the same time. W. T. Stead rightly valued these weekly meetings, but he only regarded them as pleasant periodical incidents in his magnificent plan of eventually enabling all, young and old, strong and weak, rich and poor, to get into touch with those whom they had loved, and feared that they had lost."

Serocold Skeels

"Referring to the seances with Mrs. Wriedt, which are described elsewhere, I had several sittings with her last year, and while I have yet to receive conclusive proof of the identity of the ' voices,' I had ample evidence to convince me that the phenomena were super-physical. On May 6th of this year, I attended another seance with Mrs. Wriedt, all the sitters being personal friends of Mr. Stead's, and I distinctly saw an etherialization of him, head and shoulders, with the beard slightly whiter than I remember it. I am not in the least clairvoyant and am certain that what I saw was objective.

Signed, E. R. Serocold Skeels

FROM MR. STEAD'S DEVOTED CONFIDENTIAL SECRETARY, MISS HARPER.

"My mother and I were both present on May 6th. We saw Mr. Stead, absolutely unmistakably, and heard him speak."

EDITH K. HARPER, London, May 13th. *S. A. ADELE HARPER.*

Important Certificate

Tuesday Evening, June 18th, 1912

At Mrs. Wriedt's seance to-night Mr. Stead spoke through the trumpet, clearly and with great emphasis. He greeted M. de Kerlor, reminding him of his prophecy concerning death and disaster, and saying, "I did not like to hear it at the time, but you have proved right." He encouraged M. de Kerlor to go on with the work of proving the truth of spirit return, and when the latter replied that he had sometimes doubted, but fully believed now, Mr. Stead answered with great force, "you must not say you believe, you must say you KNOW!"

Signed by the following, who were present and heard the foregoing:—E. R. Richards, W. B. Yeates, M. Jacob, S. A. Adela Harper, Nini Blom, Herbert Platt, Etta Wriedt, Wm. Blom, Ella Anker, Martin Steinsvik, W. de Kerlor, Edith Katherine Harper, Secretary, Julia's Bureau.

Letter of Estelle Stead

"I cannot do better than conclude these testimonies as to Mr. W. T. Stead's manifestations in Cambridge House, by taking an extract from a letter of Miss Estelle Stead, addressed to Mrs. Bright, of the Harbinger,[33] Melbourne.

"Miss Stead says: "The following, taken from my notes of a sitting my brother Jack and I had with Mrs. Wriedt, will, I am sure, interest you."

June 23rd—Mrs. Wriedt put out the lights, and we sat talking for a few minutes when Mrs. Wriedt started the musical box. We were all three sitting together, right away from the cabinet, in the center of the room. Presently we saw a light in the cabinet, and in a few moments we saw Father's etherealized face. It was not quite such a clear etherialization as the one I had seen before; but unmistakably Father. He seemed to be holding his hand to his face. He came right out of the cabinet over to us. He disappeared and presently we saw him again. This time he did not move from the cabinet, and the etherialization was clearer. He turned to my brother and to me and smiled. Again he disappeared; then once more we saw the dear face, and this time it came right over to us. It disappeared again and we waited a few seconds and then my brother Will spoke through the trumpet. He greeted us both and said Father would speak to us in a few moments, and we soon heard Father's dear strong voice, full of emotion, as he greeted us both. After this we talked for about half-an-hour. Sometimes Father, by his eagerness, would lose power and let the trumpet fall. Then Will would pick it up and in his calm, quiet voice would explain what had happened, and whilst Father was getting back power, my brother would talk to us. Sometimes he would turn from us and ask Father a question, and we would then hear the mumbling of the two voices, after which Will would turn to us again." Considering all that has been advanced to this stage, I can safely say, surely the evidence given of Mr. Stead's return may be accepted, and the statements made in the controls through Mrs. Coates, have been amply verified." Later on I present personal testimony verified, by seven and by fourteen sane and level-headed persons to Mr. Stead's etherializations and "direct voice," manifestations in Glenbeg House.

---

[33] *The Harbinger of Light.* The first Australian Spiritualist magazine, founded by William Terry in 1870, published monthly.

James Coates
The following experience is given by
Colonel E. R. Johnson, of 26 Aubrey Walk, Kensington

A careful and accurate observer, interested in several branches of science, he had seven sittings with Mrs. Wriedt in 1912 and twelve sittings in 1913

"During May and June I attended twelve sittings with Mrs. Wriedt at Wimbledon. I had sustained conversation with four of my relatives, some of these lasting for over half-an-hour. The total number of these amounted to sixteen. Twelve people, nearly all intimate friends, also spoke to me, and I have noted the names of twenty others who spoke. On one occasion the voices of two communicators, of Dr. Sharp and of Mrs. Wriedt, were practically speaking at the same time. The voices varied much in character, those speaking for the first time were often difficult to hear. The voices of old people, men, women and children were recognizable at once, and all improved after their first or second visit very much. English was generally used. I also heard French, Italian, Dutch, German, Servian and Croatian. Three of these languages I recognized myself. Three dogs of mine, which died some thirty years ago, came on three or four occasions. They all barked, and one was placed for a short time on my knees. Its cold nose also touched my cheek. In the 1912 sittings the color, sizes and other characteristics of these dogs were described so instantaneously that there was not the least doubt as to their identity. An Indian child named Blossom came several times. She manifested with a loud, high-pitched cry, musical and childlike. In 1912 she said that I should go to a funeral within a week. This was quite accurate—a distinguished military officer died two days after that sitting, and I witnessed the funeral six days after. At one of these 1913 sittings I had brought in my pocket a small shell with a peculiar toothed mouth, which I took out and held in my hand (room in complete darkness), asking her what it was. She first said it was a bone, but when told this was not correct she said: "A shell." Asked for further particulars, she said that it had five teeth in its mouth. I had not counted them, but the number was right. While walking round the garden at Wimbledon I found embedded in the soil a perfect paleolithic flint, evidently a harpoon head with one barb, a good many thousand years old, and as no one saw me find it, and I was careful not to show it to anyone, I could not imagine a better test. Blossom at once said: "Pooh! fishing thing!""

At one of the sittings a man, stated to be an artist and my guide, was announced. The proof he gave me was remarkable. He said he had helped me to make three sketches twenty-five years ago. I had almost forgotten them, but have since found two, and remember the third perfectly. He said that one was the sketch of an old man with a red turban.

I said: "Do you mean the old man sitting on the drum?"

"Yes," he said, "that is the one I mean, but he is not sitting on the drum. The drum was by his side, and why did you not finish that sketch?"

On examining the sketch afterwards I found that the man was sitting on a box, with the drum by his side, and that the background was left incomplete. I asked many questions as to occupations, duties, beliefs, mode of life. Here are some of the replies:

"Religion with us is one great universal one of love and beauty."

A schoolfellow, afterwards a naval officer:

> There is no reincarnation. When I rowed my boat over I did not leave my oars crossed. There are seven spheres. The idea that the lower spheres are uncomfortable is all nonsense. The realms are departments of the spheres. Supposing the sphere to be represented by a house, the rooms might indicate the realms. When I passed over I had the choice of going to higher spheres or remaining among earth conditions. I chose the latter. First arrival on the other side is not disagreeable. I was astonished and surprised at the interesting surroundings in which I found myself, but soon found that I was obliged to make my chief happiness in helping others. We can sleep if we like. I was then able to see what passed, and I saw my own body. I came back in the evening and also on the day of the funeral, where I was an unseen guest. I was not there (i.e. in the coffin), only my mortal body, which is no more than a cast-off garment. We use our eyes as you do but somewhat differently. We are able to see through objects to some extent. "

Testimony of Mr J. C. Berry, M.P.S., chemist in business at 96 Craven Park Road, Harlesden, London

He came as an entire stranger to Professor Coates at Rothesay, asking for a sitting with Mrs Wriedt. He says, under date 16th August 1913: "In the evening my wife came again, saying: "John, John, I have come back again. I have no tube in my mouth." No one in that room knew anything about my wife, children or myself. None knew that my wife died of cancer or that she had a tube in her throat. Mr. Coates adds: "Mrs Wriedt now said she saw a dog. Presently we all heard a terrier yelp. The voice told Mr Berry that this was one of the dogs that had been put to death in the discharge of his duties. Mr Berry admitted that this was correct. No one present knew that Mr Berry was a chemist until the dog yelped and Mr. Berry gave his explanation."

Mr. Stead Appears in Rothesay. James Coates/Personal Experiences

"In addition to the evidence given by those present in Cambridge House, Wimbledon, Surrey, as to the extraordinary occurrences there, I will now state my own personal experiences:—Those who discard the trance, automatic, and clairvoyant and clairaudient phenomena, as pertaining to the subjective and the region of self-deception and imagination, are appealed to by psycho-physical phenomena. In our present state a pin-prick will appeal to us when a dream-thought, however beautiful, is treated as a fancy," and discarded. But, what shall we do, when the departed appeal to us for recognition by all modes, as assuredly Mr. Stead has done? Throughout all we see the same spirit but different forms of manifestation. I will not detail here the many striking cases of etherealization and voice phenomena occurring when Mrs. Wriedt was with us, in the nine remarkable seances held in our home, but extract from my notes that which relates to Mr. Stead.

Saturday, July 13th, 8 p.m.

"Our first sitting held with Mrs. Wriedt, there appeared among other etherealizations, the face of an old aunt, our son David, Mr. Galloway's son Jack, and Mr. W. T. Stead. These were seen with more or less clearness by those to whom the "appearances" were presented. From what I have observed and from the comments of the sitters, these etherealizations have the appearance of a thin filmy cloud. The face and form—so far as seen—being thus presented. The operating intelligences present this luminous picture to some—while those at right angles to the presentation only see the luminous streak, or the edge of the cloud, next to them. Sometimes the form or cloudy likeness turns from one sitter to another, and is seen by them in turn. This happened more than once. When some cried out and said:—" Do you not see that light (or that form) Mr. Coates?" I had often to say " No." Then the light came and I saw the face. These etherealized faces, frequently appeared suddenly, moved rapidly, and then as suddenly disappeared. Although recognizable and animated appearances, they have not the definition of a painting or picture, and look more like the face of a friend looking at you through a curtain of fine white tulle or net, made visible from some emanating, inherent, luminous quality. These etherealizations are wholly objective. There is no doubt whatever that they are seen, as all external objects are, owing to the light from them acting on the eye. With this attempted explanation, I will enter more into detail as to the psycho-physical manifestations of Mr. Stead at Glenbeg House.

July 13th, about 8.20 p.m.

"There were three etherealizations in rapid succession. Each remained long enough to be recognized. Mr. Stead was one, but not so well defined as that of my old aunt. Mrs. Coates and some of those near me saw the face, but none on the opposite side of the room, and Mrs. Wriedt, the medium, did not see it—only the light. Here then, while there was not the slightest doubt in our minds, about this etherealization, it was not so clearly observed by others, to have (what I esteem of importance) sufficiently corroborating evidence by independent witnesses. Perhaps I am hard to please, but I know what the world wants. Wednesday, July 17th. At a private seance held at 2 p.m., there were only seven persons present, including the medium. These were friends most in touch with ourselves, and the sitting was private, as our children wished to communicate, and they did most effectually I will not deal with what took place, but confine myself to the manifestation of Mr. W. T. Stead.

"About 3 p.m. we were startled by his direct voice saying: "My dear Mr. Coates, you know who I am." I did as soon as I heard that voice.

I am Stead. God bless you for the work you are doing. God bless you, Mrs. Coates, for enabling me to send that message to the world. God bless all the dear friends here, may you be true—may you never be ashamed or afraid of Spiritualism. May you never forget the privileges you have received in knowing this great revelation. God grant that you may never have to suffer on its account as I have. Dear Mr. and

Mrs. Coates, I will help you. If any of you are at any time in trouble, call upon me, and I will try to be with you and help you. God bless all the dear friends and give them strength and power to make this great truth known. I am Stead, and have returned to you. God bless you, Mrs. Coates, for getting into your aura, and you Mr. Coates. Tell Mr. Robertson I have been.

I knew it was Stead, but the full and hearty tones of his greeting startled me as it did all of us. Mrs. Wriedt nearly broke down when she heard the voice, saying, "Oh, dear Mr. Stead! How good it was of you to come." We did not know then as we did since, that Mr. Stead at Julia's Bureau, directed Mrs. Wriedt to go to Julia's Bureau, directed Mrs. Wriedt to go to Rothesay as he had a message to deliver. Those present will recollect the nature of his message, which is given imperfectly above. Although there is not much of his ability there, the message is to the point. The ringing tone and conviction in his voice will not be readily forgotten.

"The following testify to the correctness of the foregoing:—Mr. and Mrs. Duncan, Edinburgh; Mrs. M'Callum, Glasgow; Miss Arrol, Mrs. Coates, Mrs. Wriedt, and the writer. Of these, Mr. and Mrs. Duncan, including ourselves, were present on the occasion when the message was received on April 26th, 1912. There was something appropriate that Mr. Duncan, of Edinburgh, who was the first to send that message to the Press, should be present when Mr. Stead addressed us in the direct voice. At the next seance—the ninth of the series, held the same day (July 17th, 8 p.m.) we had further and more striking evidence of Mr. Stead's return. Without detailing all which occurred on that occasion, which is reserved for treatment elsewhere, I will note that with reference to Mr. Stead, the following occurred:

About 9 p.m., "Dr. Sharp," Mrs. Wriedt's guide, in his usually loud staccato tones, cried out, "Mr. Duncan, as you do not see very well I want you to rise from your seat and come round to Professor Coates, so as to be nearer the cabinet."

As the room was dark, Mr. Duncan could not very well "see" how he could obey directions. "Dr. Sharp," soon solved the difficulty, by saying:—"Take the hands of those near you and pass round to where Mr. Coates is sitting," then shouting to my friend, Mr. Alexander, who is a little deaf, "Now, young man, sit in Mr. Duncan's seat, and the rest shift round. There you are, Mr. Duncan. You are seated, next Mr. Coates.?"

When Dr. Sharp was assured that all was right, he said:— "Professor Coates, I want you to rise and take a step forward. That's it." I rose and took a step forward, which brought me within a foot or eighteen inches from the front of the cabinet.

Dr. Sharp to Mr. Duncan: "Now, Mr. Duncan, take a step forward and join Mr. Coates' hand. We want to draw from you both."

What was going to happen we did not know, but certainly a cool air circulated around us, not unpleasant but distinctly felt. I suppose we were standing there one to two minutes when we were told to be seated. Mrs. Coates whispered to me that she saw the form of Mr. Stead. I looked towards the cabinet, did not see anything, but in less time than it takes to write, I heard those about me exclaim:

"There is a light at the cabinet, there's Mr. Stead." Looking up in that direction I, or rather we, saw the hazy light cloud, and the oval but indistinct face and bust of Mr. Stead, for two, perhaps three, seconds. It vanished as mysteriously as it came. A second or two afterwards, it came again, with the features, head and bust sufficiently distinct for us near at hand to observe that it was none other than Mr. Stead. The form moved, and appeared to go round the circle, bowing, as several made exclamations to that effect. And I know when Mr. Duncan, Mrs. Coates, Mr. Auld and I spoke to the effect that we recognized the face, it bowed. There was a mobile expression amounting to a smile, and the face disappeared. The shoulders were darkly visible to those near, but Mrs. Coates said she saw the whole form of which the luminous head, face, and beard were apparent to ordinary vision. Shortly after the withdrawal of this etherealization, we again heard that voice, so individualized, distinct, resonant with joy and victory:—

My dear Coates, my dear friends, God bless you all. I am Stead. You know me. You are greatly privileged in being witnesses for the great truth, that there is no death. I am not dead. Your own friends have been able to greet you here. May you have the boldness to go fearlessly forward and proclaim the glad tidings of great joy: there is no death. I am here. May you never falter or hesitate to make known the fact of spirit return. God bless you, Mrs. Coates, for giving these dear friends the opportunity they had this day of meeting with their dear ones and me. May everyone here be strengthened in all good resolves, and give to the world what they have received. God bless you, Mrs. Coates, for giving your services, without fee or reward, to the spirit-world, and Mr. Coates for his faithfulness in giving these facts to the world. God bless you all for your great and noble work.

We now understood more fully why Dr. Sharp had moved Mr. Duncan nearer to the cabinet. There was a directing mind here, and it was that of Mr. Stead himself, who wished he man who first gave his message of April 26th to the world, an opportunity to see his (Mr. Stead's) face. Owing to the physical causes mentioned, had Mr. Duncan sat where he was, he would not have seen Mr. Stead's face so clearly. Mr. Stead, as I have already mentioned, desired Mrs. Wriedt, when at Julia's Bureau, to go specially to Rothesay as he had a message to deliver. He has surely redeemed his promise. He came, and spoke in his clear and emphatic voice, compelling attention. Mr. Stead appeared delighted beyond measure, that he was able to show himself, or his simulacrum, by spirit processes, and address us in the direct voice. So far. I have only given you my testimony. If this could not be supported by the corroboration of other reputable persons, I should not have given my own."

Agnes McAllister 243, Great Western Road, Glasgow. July 22nd, 1912

"Dear Mr. Coates,—I was present on the evenings of July 13th and 17th, when Mr. Stead etherealized, and was so clearly recognized by several present. I did not know him. I heard him address you—' Mrs. Coates and the dear people present.' I authorize you to use my name in evidence for the facts."

Testimony of Councillor John Duncan (Convener of Trades, Edinburgh Town Council) and Mrs. Duncan

"Dear Mr. and Mrs. Coates,—My wife and I had great pleasure in being with you again, and having the opportunity of meeting Mrs. Wriedt in your home. The sitting at 2 p.m., July 17th, was intended to be specially for the Rothesay Circle, of a family and private nature. There were seven present. Mr. Stead spoke in his clear and deliberate way. Again at the evening sitting at which there were fourteen present the results were truly marvellous, the etherealized forms being clearly visible, although in some cases the features were not clear to me. In Mr. Stead's case I had no difficulty in recognising his features and etherealized form. He afterwards spoke for a short time in his usually emphatic and deliberate voice, but I could not commit to memory any of his remarks on this

occasion. My wife and I have no doubt, in our minds, that Mr. W. T. Stead has been able to come back to earth and give messages through Mrs. Wriedt and Mrs. Coates."
John Duncan, Margaret Duncan,
Dunearn, Granton Road, Edinburgh, 23/8/12

Testimony of Charles Walker and Elizabeth Walker, his wife. Merchant, 30, Cambridge Gardens, Pilrig, Leith

"Mr. Charles Walker and his good lady, whose formal testimony I give below, wrote me a friendly letter from Stirling, August 18th, 1912.

He says: — Dear Mr. Coates,—Neither Mrs. Walker nor myself had the pleasure of knowing and seeing Mr. Stead when in the body. From photographs his face was quite familiar to us, so that we could recognize with certainty it was Mr. Stead who, on the evening of July 17th last, at a seance held in your house, etherealized and afterwards greeted us in a loud and cheery voice. ' God bless you all.' Then followed a short address which we cannot repeat in full. He reminded us that we had been greatly privileged in receiving such beautiful proofs. He exhorted all present to go fearlessly forward telling the glad tidings of great joy, that there was no death. Finishing, he said, ' God bless you all in your great and noble work. 'Signed, *Charles Walker, Elizabeth Walker*

I will close this part with the evidence of three witnesses.

Testimony of Peter Galloway, Merchant Clothier and Outfitter, 98, Argyle Street, Glasgow, August 30th, 1912

"Dear Mr. Coates,—I have to thank you for the opportunity you so kindly gave me of being present at the seances held in your house with Mrs. Wriedt last month, and feel I cannot express the pleasure derived in being a participator in the wonderful phenomena presented.

"It is only natural that the most wonderful and satisfying part to me was, when I looked in the etherealized face of my boy. When he presented himself in front of me, I asked,

"Is that you, Jack?" The figure nodded its head, and he (Jack) confirmed my recognition by asking me through the trumpet, "What did you think of my face, father?" I cannot close this letter without mentioning the fact that Mr. Stead also spoke through the trumpet, and I saw his etherealized form.

I am, yours faithfully,

Peter Galloway

"Mr. Galloway deals with even more remarkable personal experiences—with his departed—but I refrain from producing them. I will produce them when I complete (D.V.) my treatment of the Wriedt sittings in Rothesay.'

Statement of John Auld, Engineer, Glasgow, Hazelcliffe, Ardbeg, Rothesay

This gentleman, an engineer and inventor of standing in Glasgow, sending me a report of what he saw and heard when attending the Wriedt seances in Rothesay, permits me to take the following which I think appropriate for this symposium:

"The most striking feature of the last two sittings of the series ... was the number of etheric spirit forms to be seen about the room. At the last sitting, among the first to appear was Mr. W. T. Stead, whom I at once recognized from his photographs. Mr. Stead was decidedly seen by us objectively, and his appearances were immediately followed by his voice exhorting us in strong, vigorous and natural accents to work energetically for this great truth, so satisfying to the hungry heart of humanity."

John Auld

Last known photo of the world wonder, Mrs. Etta Wriedt.

WOODLEY, Miss E. F. (English.) France-
medium in production of "Heaven's Fairy-
land," 1922.
WOODWORTH, Mrs. Bessie. (U. S.) At-
test to mediumship, see "Psychic Phenomena" (National Spiritualist, June 1, 1927, p.
6) Address: 4240 Jackson Blvd. Chicago, Ill.

WRIEDT, Mrs. Etta. Born in Oswego,
N.Y. Voice Medium, Control, "Dr. Sharp."
"The Voices" (Admiral Usborne Moore),
1913; "Spiritualism, Its History, Phenonmena
and Doctrine" (J. Arthur Hill), 1918; "Jour-
al A.S.P.R. 1924, p. 422; "Light," London,
March 28, 1925, p. 148. See "They Who Understand" (Whiting), pp. 145-146. Mrs. de
Crespigny's report (Progressive Thinker, Mar.
6, 1926, p. 1). Address: 2108 Baldwin Ave.,
Detroit, Mich.

dale), pp. 345, 355. "Psychic Research Quar-
terly" (New York), April, 1921 p. 323.
ZUGUN, Eleonore. (Roumanian.) Polter-
geist subject. Born May 24, 1913, Talpa,
Roumania. "Harry Price Investigation."
Light, June 12, 1926 —

Hartmann's Who's Who 1927 listing of Etta Wriedt's birthplace,
Oswego, New York.

IN MEMORY OF
ALBERT & MARGARET HETT
HILDAGARD
AND
ETTA WRIEDT
BY
DR. J. E. HETT

Plaque at the entrance to the auditorium at Camp Chesterfield, Indiana.

Vice Admiral William Usborne

Spirit precipitated portrait by the Bangs Sisters of Dr. Sharp, guide of Etta Wriedt.

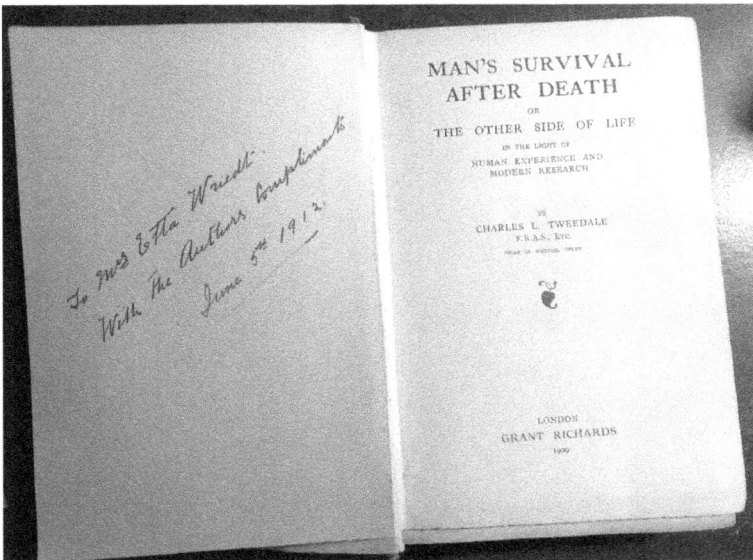

My copy of *Man's Survival After Death,* by Rev. Charles Tweedale, inscribed to Etta Wriedt, 1909.

Sir Arthur Conan Doyle.

Dr. John Sumpter King.

Spirit photo by Ada Deane of Mr. and Mrs.
Ernest Hayward sitting and daughter Cecily
manifesting.

Rev. Charles Lakeman Tweedale.

The Human Psychic
Telephone, Maud Venice
Gates.

MISS MAUD VENICE GATES,
"The Human-Psychic-Telephone."

Sir William Fletcher
Barrett.

William Thomas Stead.

ETTA'S ASTRAL BODY MANIFESTS
AND OTHER MARVELS

~

"We cannot but speak the things we have seen and heard."

~ PETER AND JOHN, ACTS IV. 20

This next little section is truly astonishing and as rare as it gets. I have never heard of these phenomena with Mrs. Wriedt or any medium I have ever researched. It is a gem of psychical experiences.

THE ASTRAL BODY OF ETTA WRIEDT MANIFESTS

Mrs. M. Jacobs

"On September 6th, the night before Mrs. Wriedt left for America, I stayed with her at the Grosvenor Hotel, as she was leaving very early the next morning for Southampton by train. She had been ill and run down with a severe cold, and I was so sorry that she was going away alone, and in bad health, that I decided to see her away. She had been

very busy packing and arranging all that day for her early departure next morning by the boat train, and went to bed tired, and fell asleep quickly. We shared the same bed (a large double bed). I could not sleep for hours, it seemed to me; and, after laying quietly for some time, I suddenly felt impressed to raise my head and look to where she was sleeping, still and quiet. What I saw made me sit right up. Over her sleeping form, her head being on the pillow partly turned away from me, was another Mrs. Wriedt, just her head and shoulders, looking full face at me over her own sleeping body, over her chest. A white, soft, gauzy scarf was loosely over the head, showing the hair, which seemed much brighter and lighter in color, the eyes intensely blue and bright, complexion clear. The eyes met mine, the face had such a sweet smile, and the expression seemed wistful. As I looked, wondering at her, the thought came into my mind: 'You do look quite beautiful, you are not as beautiful as this in life.' It was some moments before the vision faded. She was sleeping in the body peacefully through this phenomenon."
(Signed)
M. Jacob.

THE SPIRITS, STILL THEMSELVES

William Usborne Moore

"The naturalness of all that goes on is, perhaps, the feature which is most impressive. I was once talking with an uncle of mine when he stopped suddenly and exclaimed, "Tchut tchut, what was I going to say, I have dropped it," then a pause, followed by "Oh, I remember," and the voice went on as before. On another occasion I heard an old shipmate talking to a naval officer, and using some rather rough language. Suddenly something seemed to occur to him, and he said in a lower voice, "I say, Cap'n any ladies present?"

"Several" was the reply, when the spirit cried "Oh, Lord!" and was not heard again. That same evening I listened to a voice trying to identify itself to another naval officer. After repeated efforts my friend, recollecting something, said, "Oh, are you So-and-so?"

"Who the hell do you imagine has been talking to you all this time," was the unexpected reply.

"On another evening a spirit had particular difficulty in making a rather dull lady know who he was. After the lady had persistently refused to grasp his identity, the voice appeared to turn wearily round the circle, saying in a despairing tone, "Is there anyone here who can make this creature understand?" Singing familiar songs, whistling little airs and calling old nicknames are often used to bring to the sitters conviction of identity. The sole purpose of the spirit visitors appears to be to show that they are still alive. It is a passion with this gifted psychic to be the passive means of bringing children to their parents, and many scenes of the most sacred and touching character occur. Though her blank séances are about one in ten, I do not remember one sitting where the blessing of consolation for the loss of children was denied to a sorrowing father or mother."

ETTA WRIEDT IN SCOTLAND
A MERCHANT'S TESTIMONY
GLASGOW, 1912

"If the results are not the evidence of spirit return, then I am at a loss to know what could be more valuable or important." ~ William Jeffrey

William Usborne Moore

"In Scotland Mrs. Wriedt's séances were even more successful than in England. The Scotch voices of the spirits were most remarkable, especially to an English listener. Very occasionally, Gaelic was spoken. No Scotch spirit ever spoke in English unless he had lost his accent before he passed out, and no English spirit ever spoke in Scotch. I will give the record of a gentleman in Glasgow, as it is as good an instance as any I have in my notes:

"Mr. William Jeffrey, 15, Indian-street, Glasgow, keen in observation and of recognized business ability, is the sole partner in one of the largest timber and sawmill businesses in that city. He had several séances with Mrs. Wriedt. In an interview with him Mr. James Coates[34] took the following notes:

---

[34] James Coates, (1927-) British writer on Spiritualism and Spirit Photography. See: *Seeing The Invisible*, 1906; *Photographing the Invisible*, 1911. Both, outstanding books.

Mr. William Jeffrey

"I became very much interested in Mrs. Wriedt's mediumship, through reading in *Light* lately your account of the séances held in Rothesay in 1912, and determined to have some séances with her as soon as convenient. I met Mrs. Wriedt shortly after her arrival in Glasgow from London, and our first seance was held on July 2nd in my own house, 15, Indian-street, Glasgow. In addition to my people, I phoned a few others, and made up the circle. There were seventeen present, all of whom I knew to be genuine people.

"As you wish, I will not touch upon what took place as far as the other sitters were concerned, but only with that which appealed to me personally. The first voice we heard was that of my wife, who welcomed to her house all there, addressing several by name, including Mr. Galloway, Mrs. Birrell, and a visitor from London, whom (in life) she did not know. Her voice, which was quite clear, said, "O Willie, I'm awfu' glad to be here, an' speak in my home to you and these friends." My wife (who usually spoke good English, could, and often did, lapse into old Scotch ways of speaking when either very pleased or talking to intimates) addressed us in her earnest, homely, and rapid way, "I trust you will have a pleasant evening." Then she went round and spoke to each member of the family. The voice never erred when a Bella' or 'Sally' in a loving way, or prefixed 'Mr.' or 'Mrs.' to persons whom my wife would have addressed in that way in life. A voice which we recognized at once came close to me, "Bill, Bill, how are ye?"

"Who are you, friend?" I asked.

"Neil, Neil; I'm Neil, man!" followed by a hearty laugh. Neil McQuarrie was a relative by marriage, and had been for many years our cashier. He had a peculiar way of speaking, and at times was 'verra braid an' hamly,' and his laugh was not like anyone I knew. For a little he spoke to his wife, about his children, each by name. There was no mistaking his references, and his kindly expressions, designed to cheer, conveyed a world of meaning. Mrs. White, who sat next to me whispered: "Do you think he'll know me?" and immediately the answer came "Dae ye no think A ken ye, Annie White? Hoo are ye a' in London? Charlie, hoo are ye keeping? But A'm surprised to see ye here. Ye're nae sae lang-headed as Bill (myself), whom ye thocht was a wee bit off, but ye'll get something tae-night that'll convince ye."

This was so like Neil, and he followed this outburst with genial laugh. It was his laugh at this point which made the recognition unmistakable.

The voice came to me and thanked me for certain things I had done for him in life, and for his wife and child since.

"I'll not forget it, and ye'll never lose by it."

To my daughter (Mrs. Kerr) he said, "I hae tae thank ye for looking a'ter ma boys."

Mrs. Kerr: "Do you think I have been too severe in chastising them?"

"Weel, no, they're a bit self-willed an' thro' 'ither, but that is because they've nae faither to gie them bit guiding, min' that. Ye're doin' quite richt, bit lead them whiles."

Then he bid us all goodnight. My daughter 'Isa' came next, and we all had a nice little talk, and she left sending out love and kisses to us all. Another voice came, saying "Jeffrey!"

"Who are you?"

"I'm Captain George Miller's father." I said, "I did not know you."

"Well, man, I ken ye fine, an' wis wi' ye an' Captain George when ye wis on yer holidays in Orkney an' Shetland last month."

This was pretty much to the point. I asked, "What did you think of them?"

The voice: "It wasna much o' a holiday for weather, but it pit a lot o' backbone in ye." I hoped so, and said I would tell Captain George that he had been.

"Man, ye needn't fash. Ye might as well tell a log, for he will no believe ye."

"Fifteen of the seventeen sitters present received messages. I think they were satisfied, and many were delighted. Owing to my wife being able to manifest so fully through Mrs. Coates some months previously, I had looked for her to make herself known according to her promise on this occasion. Yet what took place was beyond my most sanguine anticipations. It was simply marvelous. The medium, Mrs. Wriedt, was a stranger, whom I met for the first time that morning. The seance was hurriedly convened by wire and phone, and took place in a room hastily arranged for the purpose. If the results are not evidence for spirit return, then I am at a loss to know what could be more valuable or important.

"The next séance we had was on Thursday, July 3rd, and was held in one of the rooms of the Glasgow Association of Spiritualists, Berkeley-street Hall. I got a phone asking me to come and bring a few others, as they were short of sitters. I phoned to Mrs. McMaster, and she came by putting off an engagement so that, as a visitor, her presence was wholly unexpected. This lady had never been to a seance before. The very first voice which came was that of her husband, who had passed out nine months before. He came saving, "Nellie, Nellie!" Mrs. McMasters replied, feeling it was him.

"Is that you, pa?"

"Yes, dear," was the response. I said I thought the voice was like his, and suggested that she speak freely to it.

"Yes, dear," giving kisses.

"I am so pleased to come and talk to you. You were a good lass to me. I'm so glad to see you getting on so well. Give my love to Jeffrey."

Mrs. McMasters: "You can give your love to Mr. Jeffrey yourself, for he is sitting next to me."

The voice emphatically: "No, no, I want you to give my love to my little boy, Jeffrey McMaster."

The whole of this conversation, and the circumstances under which it took place, were most telling. Before McMaster left, he said, "It was Bella" (meaning my wife in the spirit world) "brought me here," and concluded by giving his love to his wife and messages to his family.

"Mrs. Jeffrey came in her pleasant way and had a homely chat and this was followed by a word or two from my daughter Isa. There was one feature at this séance which impressed us namely, the free sprinkling of water upon us all. I mention this, too, as there was no water in the room. I did not see any, and Mr. Galloway, who had the preparation of the room, said there was none. Apart from this phenomenal the meaning of the sprinkling is, I am told, 'blessing and purification.'

"We had another sitting in the same place, Friday evening, July 4th. There were present my daughter, Mrs. Kerr, niece, and myself. My wife came and spoke for a little while to all of us. I asked, "Bella, did you like the service I had at your funeral?"

"Oh, it was very nice indeed, but" with a laugh, "the minister said far more about me than he knew." (We did not think so, as my wife in her lifetime was a good friend to anyone in sickness and distress.)

She thanked me "for the nice way you laid me to rest," and said she was "pleased to see all the folk had come to it." She finished with a little talk to us all about our affairs in a general way and some kindly counsel to myself. To my daughter, niece and myself what the voice said was conclusive.

"The seance on July 5th was attended by my daughter, son-in-law, and niece. I mention these to indicate that I am not assuming nor imagining what took place, but give their evidence. Here again my wife appeared and spoke to my daughter and Mr. Kerr. This sitting was brought to a close by the presence of a sitter asking impertinent questions about tramways and flying machines over there. The trumpet was put down with a bang, and there were no more voices that evening.

"Monday, July 7th, Berkeley-street Hall. Mrs. Kerr and I attended. I had been thinking about 'Bella,' my wife, but the first to address me was very old friend named 'Sterling,' who had departed this life some twenty years ago. I asked him who brought him here. He said, "Mrs. Jeffrey; she is helping a lot of people to come."

As he had only given his name, I said, "Are you the Mr. Sterling I knew long ago?"

"Yes," was the reply.

"Well, do you remember what was the matter with you before you died?" I asked. He answered, "I was totally blind for five years." This was correct, and a strong bit of evidence to us. Mrs. Kerr: "Have you seen Mrs. Sterling?"

"Oh, yes, dear, we are very happy here." I need not detail what was said, all was correct. Mrs. Wriedt said there was a spirit present who had shot himself. He was for Mr. Robertson, of Helensburgh.

"Did he know a man like that?"

Mr. Robertson: "Yes, he was thought to have committed suicide by shooting himself." Afterwards the voice addressed Mr. Robertson, and he, satisfied as to the identity, asked, "Did the gun go off accidentally or intentionally?"

"The voice assured him that it was an accident. "Man, I had nae need to do it" (commit suicide).

Everyone seemed to think he had, but Mr. Robertson was always of the opinion it was an accident, and what the spirit said accorded with this belief. The man had been with him a night or so before his death, and told him, among other things, how nicely everything was going on in business and other matters, he was in a cheery mood. The voice insisted that the story of his suicide was not true.

Man, I'd nae need tae destroy masel." Although this incident is not exactly personal, it so struck me, I thought I would mention it.

"My last sitting with Mrs. Wriedt in Glasgow was on Thursday, July 24th. There were eighteen present, including the medium, my daughter, son-in-law, niece, cousin and a friend. The first to speak was my wife, and after a kindly word and inquiry to each, said she was sorry that these meeting were coming to an end, and of the great comfort they had given her. I was to understand she was always with me. I asked her how it was she had spoken to me in all the sittings but one. (I had several sittings in Rothesay between July 7th and 24th.) She said it was because other relations wanted to speak to me, and I did not wish to be selfish and monopolize the time and prevent others speaking to their friends. (She had brought many to the sittings.) She finished by bidding us 'Adieu till we meet again.

"A voice purporting to be Mr. Kerr's mother spoke to us and to him. My daughter then spoke to the spirit, calling attention to the differences which had taken place between them owing to her engagement to her son. They had always been on most pleasant terms till within a short time of the marriage. The spirit answered in a clear but trembling voice, "Let bygones be bygones, dear. We will not talk about that, but you must allow for a mother's feelings when she loses her only son." All very natural and very true. "Another voice spoke, that of the late 'Mr. Kerr'-my son-in-law's father. He had been in spirit life some years. He gave us 'his crack' freely. Addressing his son, 'Charlie,' said he was "verra pleased tae sae th' business progress he was makin' in life. Many thanks tae yer 'faither-in-law fer what he's done fer ye. Ye hae had a better startin' in life by faur than ever A had."

Then addressing me, the voice said, "Thank ye, Jeffrey, for what ye hae done for me laddie, an' ther's ae thing A'll sae for him, he'll ne'er gie ye a red face."

After some friendly and kindly counsel he left. A voice saying, "Colin!"

"What Colin?"

"Colin Buchanan," and shortly afterwards, addressing Mrs. McQuarrie already referred to, touching upon some sad and private matters, which I knew were unknown to anyone in that room-never spoken of by me to my daughter or to the nearest friend. It went back into old history of forty years' standing. This was a revelation indeed. The facts unfolded were of a character which cannot with propriety be given to others. I regret that this should be the case, for it is evidence of this kind which is so convincing. To say that we were all deeply affected is the least that can be said. "Mr. Bothwell had a friend who had been drowned, who came and spoke to him. He entered into details about the fact of his passing out, which no one knew anything about.

"This gentleman was much surprised at what we had heard, as he had not believed that such communications were possible, In addition to the foregoing another voice may be mentioned, which to Mrs. McMaster. It was that of her daughter 'Serina,' who came giving this name by which she was called in life. She sent her love to all her friends, naming them one by one. She spoke particularly about her only sister, sending her a very pertinent and thoughtful message. She then came to me, and spoke to the rest of her friends, addressing each by their Christian name. There is no getting away from these facts, which came out in the presence of eighteen sitters. Everyone had a communication in that sitting, and some several. Not one of the voices that spoke that night blundered or was in error."

HE TRAVELED 6, 656 MILES FOR SITTINGS

W. Usborne Moore

"I have a friend, a mining engineer in the North of England, who is the practical head of several industries. He has been very successful in his sittings with Mrs. Wriedt. As his work prohibits him from being absent from his headquarters more than twenty-four hours at a time, he never managed to get in more than one private sitting and one general sitting on each of his visits to London. He got his rest on his return by the night mail. I find on inquiry that, during the springs and early summers of 1912 and 1913, he travelled in the aggregate no less than 6,656 miles. This, I think, will show you his earnestness in search for the truth. As he is a particularly keen and unemotional observer, I quote from his reports rather fully:

"This was the first sitting I had with Mrs. Wriedt this year, and I was uncertain as to what results I might get, but immediately the light was switched off my brother 'Jim' greeted me, and we fell into a conversation such as two brothers would who had been devoted to one another when both on this plane together. He immediately spoke of business matters, which were causing me anxiety at the time, and showed himself conversant with many of the details. Two gentlemen with whom I was closely associated in business were ill, one confined to his bed, and the other away travelling for the recovery of his health.

"After being satisfied that he had possessed himself of all the facts without my assistance, I ventured to ask my brother if he could give me an idea of what the future would bring forth concerning my two sick friends, when he said, 'Wait a few minutes, and I will take "Dr. Sharp," and he will see them and then tell you.' In the interval a sister who had passed out as a child nearly forty years ago came and spoke to me, giving her name very clearly. She correctly told me the cause of her death, and also voluntarily reminded me of some little occurrences in our child life, and went away with the parting advice that 'I was not to break my neck, as that machine thing I had went far too quickly.' (I am guilty of driving at speed on the long straight roads of the North.) 'Jim' and 'Dr. Sharp' now returned, the latter described the cause of the ill-health of my two friends in detail. The one in bed, he said, was hopeless, as he had a malignant disease, which would prove fatal in a few weeks, the other suffered from nothing more nor less than excessive cigar smoking (I knew he smoked heavily), and would be all right now for at least two years. I may say that the first case ended fatally on the last day of June, the second gentleman is now in his normal health."

FINAL WORDS

～

"What you seek is seeking you."

~ RUMI

Once again, I feel as if I have returned from a long and wondrous journey.

It is hard to put into words what it is like to explore the in-depth world of individuals who have been endowed by Nature with gifts which provided a bridge between the physical world and the world of spirits. I will never forget the thrill that ran through me when, after several years of doing research on Spiritualism, I came across the fact-which I mentioned earlier in this book-that Etta Wriedt was born in the same exact city I was born in. [35] It felt like a calling card from Etta herself and I knew then that someday I would write about her. That time has come, and now I have completed the journey for this beautiful soul.

I can say, without hesitation, that it will, in my humble opinion, stand as the definitive work on this great medium. Few people can possibly understand the depth of what this kind of work takes. I do, and so does Etta Wriedt. That, I positively know. I recognize that Admiral Usborne Moore, one of the true heroes of the truths of Spiritualism, and one whom I hold in the highest regard, has done a superlative work with

---

[35] William Hartmann, *Who's Who In Occultism, New Thought, Psychism and Spiritualism,* The Occult Press, Jamaica, New York, 1927. Where I found the information on Etta Wriedt's birthplace.

The Voices, published in 1913, and is a detailed account of numerous séances of Mrs. Wriedt. I have added to this cause by having included in my book, personal information never before published on the life of Mrs. Wriedt, photos, and additional séance memoranda. In essence, my book is a literal cousin of *The Voices.*

At times it was as if Etta was standing behind me when I was sitting here in the window typing away or documenting the séance memoranda. I have felt this sensation before with other mediums I have written about. I feel as if they are all like family members to me after all these years and I could not be more honored to bring the great work which they did into book form and send it out anyway I can into the world. It is greatly mystifying to me that what these great pioneers did, mediums and non-mediums, is so unknown by humanity in general. It seems like a great contradiction of life that the demonstrated fact of life after death, spirit return and the teachings from the hereafter which, if applied to everyday life, would assuredly being peace to the world, are mostly ignored, wholesale. Perhaps these revelations are just meant for the few, those who venture out and decide to explore and then find them. So be it.

There are many who have told me that their lives have completely changed by reading and absorbing the truths and demonstrated facts contained in my books. That is all that matters to me, even if it was one person. There will come a time when every single individual will cross the everlasting line into the spirit world. Eventually, or immediately, with no exceptions, they will be asked by a spirit guide what they had done for humanity while they existed on earth. I will feel good about my answer.

Being an archivist, I cannot help but wonder, to the depths of my soul, how William Hartmann found out that Etta was born in Oswego, New York. I guess I will have to ask him when I meet him and all the other wonderful souls in the glorious afterlife.

Peace, to all,
N. Riley Heagerty
August, 2023
Oswego, New York

SOURCES

~

These are non-archival, basic sources, many of which can found as re-prints in these modern times.

Coates, James. *Has T. T. Stead Returned?* L. N. Fowler, England, 1913

De'Crespigny, Mrs. Phillip Champion. *This World and Beyond*, Cassell and Company, London, 1934

Doyle, Arthur Conan, *The New Revelation*, Hodder and Stoughton, London 1918

Hayward, Ernest A. S. *Psychic Experiences Throughout the World*, Rider and Co., London, 1939 (Extremely rare)

King, Dr. John S. *Dawn of The Awakened Mind*, The James A. McCann Company, New York, 1920

Moore, W. Usborne, *Glimpses of The Next State*, Watts & Company, London, 1911; *The Voices, Watts & Company, London, 1913*

Tweedale, Charles L. *Man's Survival After Death*, Richards, London, 1909.

ABOUT THE AUTHOR

⌒

N. Riley Heagerty is a researcher, archivist, and author who has spent the past 30 years studying the phenomena of powerful mediums during the "Heyday of Historic Spiritualism" (1848-1950). His work has been published in 10 books, including Spectral Evidence: Volumes I, II, and III, which document extraordinary events witnessed during séances. Heagerty's mission is to bring this period of history to light and challenge the prejudice and fear that has obscured it. He believes that if the world understood Spiritualism's teachings, it would "change the course of human thinking."